DRAMAS
OF
VICTOR HUGO

MARY TUDOR
MARION DE LORME
ESMERALDA

Copyright © 2016 Read Books Ltd.
This book is copyright and may not be
reproduced or copied in any way without
the express permission of the publisher in writing

British Library Cataloguing-in-Publication Data
A catalogue record for this book is available from
the British Library

CONTENTS

Victor Hugo..7

MARY TUDOR..15
   FIRST DAY A MAN OF THE PEOPLE...................17
      SCENE I 17
      SCENE II..23
      SCENE III...29
      SCENE IV...34
      SCENE V..36
      SCENE VI...38
      SCENE VII..48
      SCENE VIII 54
      SCENE IX...55
   SECOND DAY 56
      SCENE I 57
      SCENE II..61
      SCENE III...64
      SCENE IV...66
      SCENE V..74
      SCENE VI...77
      SCENE VII..78
      SCENE VIII 85
      SCENE IX...90
   THIRD DAY PART I. WHICH OF THE TWO?..........91
      SCENE I 91
      SCENE II..95

  SCENE III.. 96
  SCENE IV.. 97
  SCENE V.. 101
  SCENE VI... 103
  SCENE VII.. 105
  SCENE VIII... 111
  SCENE IX... 113
  SCENE X.. 120
 THIRD DAY PART II.. 122
  SCENE I.. 123
  SCENE II... 127

MARION DE LORME.. **137**
 ACT I. THE MEETING.. 139
  SCENE I.. 139
  SCENE II... 146
  SCENE III.. 154
  SCENE IV... 157
 ACT II. THE ENCOUNTER..................................... 159
  SCENE I.. 159
  SCENE II... 172
  SCENE III.. 174
  SCENE IV... 179
  SCENE V.. 181
 ACT III. THE COMEDY....................................... 183
  SCENE I.. 183
  SCENE II... 188
  SCENE III.. 189
  SCENE IV... 193
  SCENE V.. 194
  SCENE VI... 196

    SCENE VII 203
    SCENE VIII 207
    SCENE IX 210
    SCENE X 211
ACT IV. THE KING 224
    SCENE I 224
    SCENE II 226
    SCENE III 227
    SCENE IV 229
    SCENE V 231
    SCENE VI 235
    SCENE VII 241
    SCENE VIII 250
ACT V. THE CARDINAL 261
    SCENE I 261
    SCENE II 263
    SCENE III 267
    SCENE IV 272
    SCENE VI 277
    SCENE VII 286

ESMERALDA **295**
    ACT I *297*
        SCENE I 297
        SCENE II 303
        SCENE III 308
    ACT II *313*
        SCENE I 313
        SCENE II 315
        SCENE III 319
        SCENE IV 322

ACT III *326*
    SCENE I 326
    SCENE II 330
    SCENE III 333
ACT IV *338*
    SCENE I 338
    SCENE II 345
    SCENE III 347
    SCENE IV 350

Victor Hugo

Victor Marie Hugo was born on 26th February 1802, in Besançon, Franche-Comté, France. He was a political campaigner, artist, poet, novelist and dramatist of the Romantic movement, considered one of the greatest French writers of all time.

Hugo's father was a freethinking republican who considered Napoléon a hero, and his mother was a Catholic Royalist, who was executed in 1812 for plotting against the legendary general. Hugo's childhood was a period of national political turmoil. Napoléon was proclaimed Emperor two years after Hugo's birth, and the Bourbon Monarchy was restored before his eighteenth birthday. The opposing political and religious views of Hugo's parents reflected the forces that would battle for supremacy in France throughout his life.

As a young man, his mother dominated his education and upbringing, and as a result Hugo's early work in poetry and fiction reflects her passionate devotion to both King and Faith. It was only later, during the events leading up to France's 1848 Revolution, that he would begin to rebel against his Catholic Royalist education and instead champion Republicanism and Freethought. Hugo was also a rebellious young man, and on falling in love with his childhood friend Adèle Foucher (1803–

1868), became secretly engaged against his mothers wishes. Because of his close relationship with his mother, Hugo waited until after his mother's death (in 1821) to marry Adèle in 1822.

Hugo published his first novel the year following his marriage (*Han d'Islande*, 1823), and his second three years later (*Bug-Jargal*, 1826). Between 1829 and 1840 he would publish five more volumes of poetry, cementing his reputation as one of the greatest elegiac and lyric poets of his time. Victor Hugo's first mature work of fiction appeared in 1829, and reflected the acute social conscience that would infuse his later work. *The Last Day of a Condemned Man* would have a profound influence on later writers such as Albert Camus, Charles Dickens, and Fyodor Dostoevsky. It was soon followed by *The Hunchback of Notre-Dame* (in 1831), which was quickly translated into other language across Europe.

Adèle and Victor Hugo had their first child, Léopold, in 1823, but the boy died in infancy. The following year, on 28th August 1824, the couple's second child, Léopoldine was born, followed by Charles in 1826, François-Victor in 1828, and Adèle in 1830. Hugo's oldest and favourite daughter, Léopoldine, died at the age of nineteen in 1843, shortly after her marriage to Charles Vacquerie. On 4th September 1843, she drowned in the Seine at Villequier, pulled down by her heavy skirts, when a boat overturned. Her young husband also died trying to save her. The death left her father devastated; Hugo was travelling with his mistress at the time in the south of France, and first learned about Léopoldine's death from a newspaper he read in a cafe.

Hugo wrote many poems about his daughter's tragic life and death, and many biographers have claimed that he never completely recovered from this traumatic incident. His most famous poem is probably *Demain, Dès L'aube*, in which he describes visiting her grave. He began planning a major novel about social misery and injustice as early as the 1830s, but it would take a full seventeen years for *Les Misérables* to be realized and finally published in 1862. On its publication, the critical establishment was generally hostile to the novel, with Gustave Flaubert claiming he found within it 'neither truth nor greatness' and Baudelaire castigating it as 'tasteless and inept.' Despite this, *Les Misérables* was a massive hit with the public, and today remains Victor Hugo's most enduringly popular work.

After three unsuccessful attempts, Hugo was finally elected to the Académie Française in 1841, solidifying his position in the world of French arts and letters. He was also elevated to the peerage by King Louis-Philippe in the same year and entered the Higher Chamber as a *pair de France*, where he spoke against the death penalty and social injustice, and in favour of freedom of the press and self-government for Poland. In 1848, Hugo was elected to the Parliament as a conservative. In 1849 he broke with the conservatives when he gave a noted speech calling for the end of misery and poverty. When Louis Napoleon (Napoleon III) seized complete power in 1851, establishing an anti-parliamentary constitution, Hugo openly declared him a traitor to France.

Hugo decided to live in exile after Napoleon III's coup d'état at the end of 1851. After leaving France, he lived in Brussels briefly in 1851, before moving to the Channel Islands, first to Jersey (1852–1855) and then to the smaller island of Guernsey in 1855, where he stayed until 1870. Whilst in exile, Hugo published his famous political pamphlets against Napoleon

III, *Napoléon le Petit* and *Histoire d'un Crime*, which whilst banned in France, had a strong impact. Although Napoleon III proclaimed a general amnesty in 1859, the author stayed in exile, only returning when Napoleon was forced from power in 1870. Hugo's next novel, *Troilers of the Sea* turned away from the social and political themes so prevalent in *Les Miserables*. It told the story of a man hoping to gain the approval of his beloved's father by rescuing his ship - thus battling the elements, mythical beasts and the sea itself. It was published in 1866, and was dedicated to the channel islands, in which Hugo found such a welcoming home.

Hugo returned to political and social issues in his next novel, *The Man Who Laughs*, which was published in 1869 and painted a critical picture of the aristocracy. The novel was not as successful as his previous efforts, and Hugo himself began to comment on the growing distance between himself and literary contemporaries such as Flaubert and Émile Zola, whose realist and naturalist novels were now exceeding the popularity of his own work. After the Siege of Paris, Hugo lived again in Guernsey from 1872 to 1873, before finally returning to France for the remainder of his life. His last novel, *Ninety-Three*, published in 1874, dealt with a subject that Hugo had previously avoided: the Reign of Terror during the French Revolution. Though Hugo's popularity was on the decline at the time of its publication, many now consider *Ninety-Three* to be a work on par with his earlier and better-known novels.

When Hugo returned to Paris in 1870, the country hailed him as a national hero. This was a sad time for the ageing writer however, as within a brief period he suffered a mild stoke, his daughter Adèle's internment in an insane asylum, and the death of his two sons. His wife Adèle had died in 1868. Hugo's mistress, Juliette Drouet, also died in 1883 – two years before Hugo's own death. Despite this, to honour the fact that he was entering his eightieth year, in 1882, one of the greatest tributes to a living writer was held. The celebrations began on 25th June when Hugo was presented with a Sèvres vase, the traditional gift for sovereigns, and on 27th June one of the largest parades in French history was held.

Victor Hugo's death from pneumonia on 22nd May 1885, at the age of eighty-three, generated intense national mourning. He was not only revered as a towering figure in literature, but he was also a statesman who shaped the Third Republic and democracy in France. More than two million people joined his funeral procession in Paris from the Arc de Triomphe to the Panthéon, where he was buried. He shares a crypt within the with Alexandre Dumas and Émile Zola.

THE RENDEZVOUS.

MARY TUDOR

DRAMATIS PERSONÆ

- Mary, The Queen.
- Jane.
- Gilbert.
- Fabiano Fabiani.
- Simon Renard.
- Joshua Farnaby.
- A Jew.
- Lord Clinton.
- Lord Chandos.
- Lord Montague.
- Master Eneas Dulverton.
- Lord Gardiner.
- A Jailer.

Lords, Pages, Guards, the Executioner.
LONDON, 1553.

MARY TUDOR

FIRST DAY

A MAN OF THE PEOPLE

SCENE.—*Border of the Thames. A deserted strand. An old parapet in ruins, conceals the borders of the water. To the right, a house of mean appearance. At the corner of this house, a statuette of the Virgin, at whose feet burns a wick in an iron lattice. In the background, beyond the Thames, London. Two high buildings are seen—the Tower of London and Westminster. The sun is setting*

SCENE I

Several men are grouped here and there on the Strand, among whom are SIMON RENARD, JOHN BRIDGES, BARON CHANDOS, ROBERT CLINTON, ANTHONY BROWN, VISCOUNT OF MONTAGUE

LORD CHANDOS.

You are right, my lord, this damned Italian must have bewitched the Queen. She can't exist without him; she lives only for him, finds pleasure only in him, listens only to him. If a day passes without seeing him, her eyes droop as they did when she loved Cardinal Polus, you remember?

SIMON RENARD.

She is very much in love, it is true, and, consequently, very jealous.

LORD CHANDOS.

The Italian has bewitched her.

LORD MONTAGUE.

For a fact, they say that people of his nationality have philters for that purpose.

LORD CLINTON.

The Spanish are clever at poisons which kill people, the Italians are clever at poisons which make people fall in love.

LORD CHANDOS.

Then Fabiani is Spanish and Italian, at the same time. The Queen is in love and is ill. He has made her drink both.

LORD MONTAGUE.

As to that, is he really Spanish or Italian?

LORD CHANDOS.

It appears certain that he was born in Italy, in the Capitanate, and that he was brought up in Spain. He claims to be connected with a great Spanish family. Lord Clinton has the story at his finger-tips.

LORD CLINTON.

An adventurer—neither Spanish nor Italian, and still less English, thank God! These men without a country have no pity on a country, when they become powerful.

LORD MONTAGUE.

Didn't you say the Queen was ill, Chandos? That does not hinder her from leading a very gay life with her favorite!

LORD CLINTON.

A gay life! A gay life! The people weep while the Queen laughs and the favorite is gorged. This man eats silver and drinks gold! The Queen has given him the estates of Lord Talbot, the great Lord Talbot! The Queen has made him Earl of Clanbrassil and Baron of Dinasmonddy, this Fabiano Fabiani who says he belongs to the Spanish family of Peñalver, and who lies when he says it. He is an English peer like you, Montague, like you, Chandos, like Stanley, like Norfolk, like myself, like the King! He has the garter, the same as the Infante of Portugal, as the King of Denmark, as Thomas Percy, seventh Earl of Northumberland. And what a tyrant is this tyrant who rules us from his bed! Never did such a curse rest upon England! And yet I have seen much—I, who am old! There are seventy new gallows at Tyburn; the stakes are always embers and never ashes; the executioner's ax is sharp every morning and blunted every night. Every day some great nobleman is slaughtered; the day before yesterday it was Blantyre, yesterday Northcurry, to-day South-Reppo, to-morrow Tyrconnel. Next week it will be you, Chandos, and next month it will be I. My lords, my lords, it is shameful and outrageous that all these honest English heads should fall to please a miserable adventurer who does not even belong to our country! It is a frightful and unbearable thing, to think that a Neapolitan favorite can drag as many blocks as he likes from under this Queen's bed. These two lead a gay life, you say? By Heaven, it is infamous! Ah, they lead a gay life, these lovers, while the headsman, at their door, makes widows and orphans! Oh, their Italian guitar is too well accompanied by the clank of chains! Madame Queen! you send to the chapel of Avignon for your singers; every day in your palace, you have comedies, plays, and a stage crowded with musicians! Upon my life, madame, less joy at your house and less mourning at ours, if you please; fewer dancers there, and fewer executioners here; fewer farces at Westminster, and fewer scaffolds at Tyburn!

LORD MONTAGUE.

Have a care, my Lord Clinton! We are loyal subjects! Not a word against the Queen, everything against Fabiani.

SIMON RENARD (*laying his hand on* Lord Clinton's *shoulder*).

Have patience!

LORD CLINTON.

Patience! That is easy enough for you to say, Mr. Simon Renard! You are bailiff of Amont in Franche-Comte, subject of the Emperor, and his embassador at London. You represent the Prince of Spain, the Queen's future husband. Your person is sacred to the favorite. But it is different with us. You see, for you, Fabiani is the lover; for us he is the butcher! [*It is night.*

SIMON RENARD.

This man troubles me as much as you! You tremble only for your life. I tremble for my power. That means much more. I do not talk; I act. I feel less anger than you, perhaps, but I feel more hate. I will destroy the favorite.

LORD MONTAGUE.

Yes! but how to do it! I think of it all day.

SIMON RENARD.

It is not in the daytime that the favorites of queens are made and unmade; it is at night.

LORD CHANDOS.

This night is dark and frightful.

SIMON RENARD.

I find it good for what I wish to do.

LORD CHANDOS.

What do you mean to do?

SIMON RENARD.

You shall see. My Lord Chandos, when a woman reigns, caprice reigns. Politics are no longer a matter of calculation then, but of chance. You can count upon nothing. To-day does not logically bring to-morrow. Public affairs are no longer like a game of chess, but a game of cards.

LORD CLINTON.

That is all very well; but let us come to the point. When will you deliver us from the favorite? Time is pressing. To-morrow Tyrconnel will be beheaded.

SIMON RENARD.

If I find the man I am looking for, to-night, Tyrconnel will sup with you to-morrow.

LORD CLINTON.

What do you mean? What will have become of Fabiani?

SIMON RENARD.

Have you good eyes, my lord?

LORD CLINTON.

Yes, although I am old and the night is dark.

SIMON RENARD.

Do you see London on the other side of the water?

LORD CLINTON.

Yes. Why?

SIMON RENARD.

Look well! From here you can see the height and the depth of every favorite's fortune—Westminster and the Tower of London.

LORD CLINTON.

Well?

SIMON RENARD.

If God is with me, there is a man who at this moment is yet there [*pointing to Westminster*], and who to-morrow, at the same time, will be here [*pointing to the Tower*].

LORD CLINTON.

Pray God be with you!

LORD MONTAGUE.

The people hate him no less than we do. What a festival will his fall make in London!

LORD CHANDOS.

We have placed ourselves in your hands, Sir Bailiff. Dispose of us. What must we do?

SIMON RENARD (*indicating a house, near to the water*).

You all see that house. It is the house of Gilbert the engraver. Do not lose sight of it. Now go away with your people, but don't go too far. Above all, do nothing without me.

LORD CHANDOS.

It is agreed. [*They all exit at different sides.*

SIMON RENARD (*alone*).

The man I need is not easy to find.

[*He exits.* Jane *and* Gilbert *enter, arm in arm; they go toward the house.* Joshua Farnaby, *enveloped in a long cloak, accompanies them.*

SCENE II

JANE, GILBERT, JOSHUA FARNABY

JOSHUA.
I must leave you here, my good friends. It is midnight, and I must go back to my post of turnkey of the Tower of London. I am not as free as you are, you see! A turnkey is only another kind of prisoner! Good-by, Jane! Good-by, Gilbert. Ah, my friends, how glad I am to see you happy! When is the wedding, Gilbert?

GILBERT.
In one week, isn't it, Jane?

JOSHUA.
Faith! day after to-morrow is Christmas. This is the day of good wishes and presents. But I have nothing to wish you. It would be impossible to wish more beauty to the bride or more love to the bridegroom. You are fortunate.

GILBERT.
Good Joshua! And you, are you not happy?

JOSHUA.
Neither happy nor unhappy. As for me, I have given up everything. Look you, Gilbert [*opening his cloak and disclosing a bunch of keys hanging to his belt*], prison keys

always jingling at your side, talk to you, suggest all sorts of philosophical ideas to you. When I was young, I was like the rest—in love for a day, ambitious for a month, mad a whole year. It was during the reign of Henry VIII. that I was young. Strange man that Henry VIII.! A man who changed his wives as a woman changes her dresses. He repudiated the first, had the second beheaded, had the third's womb cut open; as for the fourth, he had mercy on her—he sent her off; but for revenge he had the fifth's head cut off! This isn't the story of Bluebeard I am telling you, my beautiful Jane; it is the history of Henry VIII. In those days I interested myself in the religious wars; I fought first for one side and then for the other. That was the wisest thing to do. The whole business was very ticklish. It was whether to be for or against the Pope. The King's officers hanged those who were for, but they burned those who were against. The neutral people—those who neither were for nor against—they hanged them or they burned them indiscriminately. We managed as we could. Yes, the rope; no, the fagot. I, who am speaking to you, I smelled of burning very often, and I am not sure that I was not un-hanged two or three times. Those were great times; very much like the times now. The devil take me if I know now whom I fought for or what I fought about. If people speak to me now about Master Luther and Pope Paul III., I shrug my shoulders. You see, Gilbert, when a man has gray hairs he shouldn't go back to the opinions he fought for nor the women he loved when he was twenty. The women and the opinions will seem very ugly, very old, very paltry, very silly, very much wrinkled and out of date. Such is my history. Now I am through with public affairs. I am no longer the King's soldier nor the Pope's soldier; I am jailer of the Tower of London. I don't fight any more for anybody, and I put everybody under lock and key. I am turnkey and I am old. I have one foot in a prison and the other in the grave. I am the one who picks up the remnants of all the ministers and favorites who go to pieces in the Queen's palace. It is very amusing. I have also a little child whom I love, and you both whom I love too; and if you are happy, I am happy also.

GILBERT.

If that is the case, you can be happy; can't he, Jane?

JOSHUA.

I can't do anything to add to your happiness, but Jane can do everything. You love her. I may never be able to do anything for you. Fortunately for you, you are not high and mighty enough to ever need the help of the turnkey of the Tower of London. Jane will pay my debt at the same time that she pays her own, because she and I owe everything to you. Jane was but a poor child, a forsaken orphan; you took her home and brought her up. I was drowning in the Thames, one fine day, and you dragged me out of the water.

GILBERT.

Why do you always talk about that, Joshua?

JOSHUA.

In order to tell you that our duty, Jane's and mine, is to love you. I, as a brother; and she, not as a sister.

JANE.

No, as a woman. I understand you, Joshua. [*She sinks back into her reverie.*

GILBERT.

Look at her, Joshua! Is she not beautiful and attractive, and is she not worthy of a king? If you only knew! You cannot imagine how I love her!

JOSHUA.
Be careful! It is dangerous. A woman should not be loved so much as that. With a child, it is different.

GILBERT.
What do you mean?

JOSHUA.
Nothing. I will be at your wedding next week. I hope State affairs will leave me a little liberty then, and that everything will be finished.

GILBERT.
How? What will be finished?

JOSHUA.
Ah, these things do not interest you, Gilbert. You are in love; you belong to the people. What do the intrigues of the high-born matter to you, who are happy among the low-born? But since you ask me, I will tell you that within one week, perhaps within twenty-four hours, it is hoped that Fabiano Fabiani's place near the Queen will be filled by another.

GILBERT.
Who is Fabiano Fabiani?

JOSHUA.
The Queen's lover: a very celebrated and a very fascinating favorite—a favorite who has had his enemies' heads chopped off with greater dispatch than a procuress can repeat an "Ave"; the best favorite that the executioner of the Tower of London has had for ten years. For you must know that every great lord's head that falls, brings in ten silver crowns to the executioner—sometimes twice as much, when the head is

very distinguished. The fall of this Fabiani is greatly desired; though, I must say, during my duties at the Tower, it is only the bad-tempered people whom I hear find fault with him—the discontented people; those whose heads are to fall next month.

GILBERT.

Let the wolves rend each other! What do we care about the Queen and the Queen's favorite? Isn't it so, Jane?

JOSHUA.

There is a big conspiracy against Fabiani; if he escapes, he will be lucky. I should not be surprised if they were to strike some blow to-night. I just saw Master Simon Renard prowling about here, very much absorbed.

GILBERT.

Who is Master Simon Renard?

JOSHUA.

Is it possible that you don't know? He is the Emperor's right hand at London. The Queen is to marry the Prince of Spain, and Simon Renard is his embassador to her. The Queen hates him, this Simon Renard; but she is afraid of him, and she can't do anything to him. He has already destroyed two or three favorites. It seems to be his instinct to destroy favorites. He clears up the palace from time to time. He is a shrewd and spiteful man; he knows all that goes on, and he digs two or three subterranean rows of intrigues under every event. As for Lord Paget—didn't you ask me who was Lord Paget?—he is a crafty nobleman who helped to manage affairs under Henry VIII. He is a member of the secret council. He has such an ascendency that the other ministers do not dare to breathe in his presence—except, however, the chancellor, my Lord Gardiner, who detests him. A violent man, this Gardiner, and well born. As for Paget, he was nobody—a cobbler's son. He is to be made Baron Paget of Beaudesert in Stafford.

GILBERT.

How glibly he tells all these things, this Joshua.

JOSHUA.

My faith! It's from hearing the prisoners of State talk.

[Simon Renard *appears at the back of stage.*

You see, Gilbert, the man who knows most about the history of these times is the turnkey of the Tower of London.

Simon Renard (*who overhears these last words*).

You are mistaken, my master; it is the executioner!

JOSHUA (*low to* Gilbert *and* Jane).

Let us move back a little!

[Simon Renard *goes off slowly; when he has disappeared.*

That is Master Simon Renard himself.

GILBERT.

I don't like to have all these men prowling about my house.

JOSHUA.

What the devil is he doing here? I must hurry back; I think he is getting work ready for me. Good-by, Gilbert! Good-by, my beautiful Jane, I knew you when you were no bigger than that, all the same!

GILBERT.

Good-by, Joshua! What are you hiding there under your cloak?

JOSHUA.

I've got my conspiracy, too!

GILBERT.

What conspiracy?

JOSHUA.

O lover who forgets everything else! I have just reminded you that the day after to-morrow is the time for Christmas presents. The nobles are plotting a surprise for Fabiani. Well, I am plotting a surprise too. The Queen may give herself the present of a brand-new favorite. I am going to give my child a doll. [*He takes a doll from his cloak.*] Brand-new, too! We will see which will be the first to break her toy. God keep you, my friends.

GILBERT.

Good-by, Joshua!

[Joshua *departs*. Gilbert *takes* Jane's *hand and kisses it with passion.*

JOSHUA (*from back of stage*).

How wise is Providence! She gives to each one his plaything. The doll to the child, the child to the man, the man to the woman, and the woman to the devil. [*Exits.*

SCENE III

GILBERT, JANE

GILBERT.

I must go, too. Good-by, Jane: sleep well.

JANE.

You are not coming in with me to-night, Gilbert?

GILBERT.

I can't. You know, I told you before, Jane, I have some work to do in my shop to-night. I must engrave the handle of a dagger for some Lord Clanbrassil, whom I have never seen, and who wants it to-morrow morning.

JANE.

Then good-night, Gilbert. Until to-morrow!

GILBERT.

No, Jane, wait a moment. Heaven! how it hurts me to leave you, even for a few hours. How true it is that you are my life and my joy. Yet I have to work—we are so poor. I won't go in, because I should stay; and yet I can't leave you, weak man that I am. Let us sit down by the door a few moments, on this bench. I think it will be easier to go from here than if I went into the house, and, above all, into your room. Give me your hand.

[*He sits and takes her hands in his; she stands.*

Jane, do you love me?

JANE.

Oh, I owe you everything, Gilbert. I know it, although you have concealed it from me a long time! When I was little, almost in my cradle, my parents abandoned me, and you took me. For sixteen years your hand has worked for me as if you were a father; your eyes have watched over me like a mother. What would I be without you, just Heaven! All I have, you have given me; all I am, you have made me.

GILBERT.

Jane, do you love me?

JANE.

What devotion yours has been, Gilbert! You work for me,

night and day; you wear your eyes out, you kill yourself for me. You are going to sit up all night again to-night. And never a reproach to me, never an unkindness, never an angry word! You are very poor, yet you remember all my small womanly vanities; you gratify them. Gilbert, whenever I think about you, my eyes fill with tears. You have often gone without bread; I have never gone without my ribbons.

GILBERT.

Jane, do you love me?

JANE.

Gilbert, I would like to kneel down and kiss your feet.

GILBERT.

Do you love me, do you love me? All that does not prove that you love me. I want that word, Jane! Gratitude, always gratitude! Oh, I stamp it underfoot, your gratitude. I want love or nothing! Die! Jane, you have been my daughter for sixteen years; now you are to be my wife. I adopted you; now I am to marry you—in one week. You know, you promised me; you have consented; you are my betrothed. You loved me when you promised that. Oh, Jane, there was a time—do you remember it?—when you told me, "I love you," and you lifted your sweet eyes to heaven. That is the way I want you to be. For some months now, you have seemed different, especially during these last three weeks that my work has kept me away from here nights. Jane, I must have you love me! I am used to it. You were always so light-hearted; now you are sad and absent-minded—not cold, my poor child (you try your best not to be), but I feel your loving words do not come as tenderly and as naturally as they used. What is the matter? Don't you love me any more? I know I am an honest man, I know I am a good workman; but I would rather be a robber and an assassin, and be loved by you. Jane, if you knew how much I love you!

JANE.

I know it, Gilbert, and it makes me weep.

GILBERT.

For joy, isn't it? Say it is for joy! Oh, I need to believe it. There is only that in the world—to be loved. I have only a poor workingman's heart, but my Jane must love me. Why do you always talk to me about what I have done for you? One single word of love from you puts all the gratitude on my side. I will damn myself and commit a crime, whenever you wish it. You will be my wife, won't you, and you love me? Oh, Jane, for one look of your eyes I would give my work and my labor; for one smile, my life; for one kiss, my soul.

JANE.

What a noble heart you have, Gilbert.

GILBERT.

Listen to me, Jane—laugh at me if you will; I am mad, I am jealous! I will tell you why. Do not get angry! It seems to me, for some time I have seen several young lords prowling around here. Do you know, Jane, I am thirty-two years old. For a poor, clumsy, badly-dressed workman like myself, who am no longer young, who am not handsome, what a misery it is to love a charming, beautiful girl of seventeen, who attracts all the handsome, gold-bedizened young nobles around her, as a light attracts the butterflies. Oh, I suffer; indeed, I do! But I never blame you, even in my thoughts! You, so honest, so pure; you, whose brow has never been touched, except by my lips. I only feel, sometimes, that you look on the Queen's cavalcades and retinues with too much pleasure, that you enjoy too much the fine suits of velvet and satin, under which there are no hearts, no souls. Forgive me. My God! why do so many young noblemen come around here? Why am I not handsome, young, noble, rich? Gilbert the engraver—that is all I am! They are Lord Chandos, Lord Gerard Fitz-Gerard, Earl of Arundel, the Duke of Norfolk! Oh, how I hate them! I spend my life engraving the handles of their swords, which I would like to plunge into their bowels.

JANE.

Gilbert!

GILBERT.

I beg your pardon, Jane! Love makes us very wicked, doesn't it?

JANE.

No, very good; for you are good, Gilbert.

GILBERT.

Oh, how much I love you! It increases every day. I would like to die for you! Love me or not, you can do as you please. I am mad. Forgive all that I have said. It is late: I must leave you! Good-by! Oh, how I hate to leave you! Go in! Haven't you your key?

JANE.

No; I haven't had it for several days.

GILBERT.

Take mine. Until to-morrow morning! Jane, don't forget this! To-day I am still your father: in one week I shall be your husband.

[*He kisses her on the forehead and exits.*

JANE (*alone*).

My husband! Oh, no! I will never commit that crime. Poor Gilbert! he loves me truly; and the other—ah, provided I have not preferred vanity to love! Unhappy woman that I am, into whose power have I fallen! Oh, I am most thankless and most guilty! I hear footsteps! Let me get in quickly. [*Goes into house.*

SCENE IV

GILBERT, A MAN *enveloped in cloak and wearing a yellow cap.* THE MAN *holds* GILBERT *by the hand*

GILBERT.

Yes, I recognize you; you are the Jewish beggar who has been prowling around this house for several days. What do you want with me? Why have you taken hold of my hand, and why have you brought me back here?

THE MAN.

Because what I have to say to you, I can only say here.

GILBERT.

Well, what is it? Speak! Hurry!

THE MAN.

Listen, young man. One night, sixteen years ago, Lord Talbot, Earl of Waterford, was beheaded by torchlight, for the crimes of popery and rebellion, while his followers were cut to pieces in the city of London by Henry VIII.'s soldiers. They shot in the streets all night. That night a very young workman, who was much more interested in his labor than in the battle, was working in his stall. It was the first stall from the entrance of London Bridge; a low door on the right, the remains of some old red paint on the wall. It might have been two o'clock in the morning. They were fighting all around there. The balls hissed across the Thames. Suddenly some one knocked at the door of the stall, through which the workman's lamp threw a glimmer. The workman opened it. A man he did not know, entered. This man carried in his arms a baby in long clothes, who was much frightened and was crying. The man put the child down on the table and said, "Here is a creature who has neither father nor mother." Then he went out slowly and closed the door after him. Gilbert, the workman, had neither father nor mother himself. The workman accepted the child: the orphan adopted the orphan. He took it, watched over it, clothed it, fed it, tended it, brought it up, loved it. He gave himself entirely to this poor little creature whom civil war had thrown into his stall. He forgot everything for her—his youth, his love-affairs, his pleasures; he made this child the sole object of his work, his affections, his life: and it has lasted sixteen years. Gilbert, the workman was you; the child—

GILBERT.

Was Jane. All that you say is true; but what are you driving at?

THE MAN.

I forgot to say that on the child's swaddling-clothes a paper was pinned, on which was written: "Have pity upon Jane."

GILBERT.

It was written in blood. I have kept that paper. I always carry it about me. But you torture me. What is your purpose, tell me.

THE MAN.

This. You see that I am acquainted with your affairs. Gilbert, watch over your house to-night.

GILBERT.

What do you mean?

THE MAN.

Not another word. Don't go to your work; stay around the house: watch! I am neither your friend nor your enemy; this is only a piece of advice that I give you. Now, for your own sake, leave me! Go down that side, and come back if you hear me call for help.

GILBERT.

What does this mean? [*Goes off slowly.*

SCENE V

THE MAN (*alone*).

The matter is well arranged now. I needed some one young and strong to help me if it was necessary. This Gilbert is just the man I want. I think I hear the sound of oars and a guitar on the water. Yes.

[*He goes to the parapet. A guitar and distant singing are heard.*

> When you sing soft at night, love,
> Clasped in my arms so fond,
> Can you not hear the tender thoughts
> Which to your voice respond?

Your song brings back unto my heart
The happy days of yore;
Then sing, my beauty, sing, my love,
Sing on for evermore!

THE MAN.

That is my man!

[*The voice draws nearer with each verse.*

When you laugh, on your lips, dear,
Love's sweetest shadows play;
And doubt and cruel unbelief
Are sudden chased away.
For laughter proves we're loyal
And faithful to the core;
Then laugh, my beauty, laugh, my love,
Laugh on for evermore!

When you sleep, calm and pure, love,
In shadow, 'neath my eyes,
And your soft breathing gives my heart
Its tenderest replies,
On your sweet form my eyes can feast,
Oh, beauty's priceless store!
Then sleep, my beauty, sleep, my love,
Sleep on for evermore!

And when you say, "I love you,"

In truth it seems to be
As if God's heaven were opening
Especially for me.
I see dreams hidden in your eyes
That we've not dreamed before;
Then love me, oh, my beauty,
Love me for evermore!

You see, the whole of life, dear,
Lies in those words, just four—
All things that people envy,
All things that men adore,
All things that are seductive,
On which our heart sets store.
To sing, to laugh, my beauty,
To sleep, to love, no more!

THE MAN.
He lands! Good! He sends off the boatmen. Excellent!
[*Comes back to the front of the stage.*
Here he comes.
[Fabiano Fabiani *enters, enveloped in a cloak; he goes toward the door of the house.*

SCENE VI

The Man, Fabiano Fabiani

THE MAN (*stopping* Fabiani).

A word with you, if you please.

FABIANI.

I believe some one is speaking to me. Who is this knave? Who are you?

THE MAN.

Whatever you wish me to be.

FABIANI.

This lantern is not very bright, but you wear a yellow cap, it seems to me—a Jew's cap. Are you a Jew?

THE MAN.

Yes, a Jew. I have something to tell you.

FABIANI.

What is your name?

THE MAN.

I know your name, and you don't know mine. I have the advantage. Permit me to keep it.

FABIANI.

You know my name? That isn't true.

THE MAN.

I know your name. At Naples you were called Signor Fabiani; at Madrid, Don Fabiano; at London you are called Lord Fabiano Fabiani, Earl of Clanbrassil.

FABIANI.

The devil take you!

THE MAN.

God keep you!

FABIANI.

I will have you cudgeled. I do not wish my name to be known when I go abroad by night.

THE MAN.

Especially when you go where you are going.

FABIANI.

What do you mean?

THE MAN.

If the Queen knew!

FABIANI.

I am going nowhere in particular.

THE MAN.

Oh, yes, my lord! You are going to see the fair Jane, the betrothed of Gilbert the engraver.

FABIANI (*aside*).

The devil! This is a dangerous man.

THE MAN.

Shall I tell you more? You have seduced this girl, and during the last month she has received you twice in her house at night. This is the third time. The beauty is waiting for you.

FABIANI.

Keep still. Do you want hush-money? How much do you want?

THE MAN.

We will see about that by-and-by. Now, my lord, shall I tell you why you have seduced this girl?

FABIANI.

By my faith! because I was in love with her.

THE MAN.

No. You were not in love with her.

FABIANI.

I wasn't in love with Jane.

THE MAN.

No more than with the Queen! Love, oh, no! calculation, yes.

FABIANI.

Why, fool, you are no man at all! You are my conscience dressed up like a Jew.

THE MAN.

I will speak to you as if I were your conscience. This is your plan. You are the Queen's favorite. The Queen has given you the garter, an earldom, and a lordship—empty things, all of them. The garter is a rag; the earldom is a word; the lordship is the right to have your head cut off. You wanted something more. You wanted fine lands, fine bailiwicks, fine castles, fine revenues in fine English pounds. Well, King Henry VIII. confiscated the estates of Lord Talbot, who was beheaded sixteen years ago. You got Queen Mary to give you Lord Talbot's estates. But, to make the gift valid, it is necessary that Lord Talbot should have died without heirs. And since Lord Talbot died for Queen Mary and for her mother, Catherine of Aragon, since Lord Talbot was a Papist, and since the Queen is a Papist, it is not at all doubtful, if there existed such an heir or an heiress, that Queen Mary would take back the estates from you, great favorite though you are, and out of duty, gratitude and religion, return them to the heir or heiress. You were quite easy on that score, for Lord Talbot had never had but one little daughter; she disappeared from her cradle at the time of her father's execution, and all England believed her to be dead. But your spies have lately discovered that during the night in which Lord Talbot and his partisans were exterminated by Henry VIII., a child was mysteriously brought to an engraver on London Bridge, and that it was probable that this child, reared under the name of Jane, was Jane Talbot, the little girl who had disappeared. It is true that the written proofs of her birth were lacking, but they might be found any day. The discovery was unpleasant. It would be hard to see one's self forced some day to give back Shrewsbury, Wexford, which is a fine city, and the magnificent earldom of Waterford, to a little girl! What was to be done? You searched for a way to set aside this young girl, and to destroy her. An honest man would have had her killed or poisoned. You, my lord, have done better—you have dishonored her.

FABIANI.

Insolent fool!

THE MAN.

It is your conscience which is speaking, my lord. Another man would have taken this young girl's life; you have taken her honor, and, consequently, her future. Queen Mary is a prude, although she has lovers herself.

FABIANI.

This man goes to the bottom of everything.

THE MAN.

The Queen's health is bad; the Queen may die, and then you, the favorite, will fall shattered on her tomb. The actual proofs of this young girl's rank may be found; and then, if the Queen is dead, Jane Talbot, dishonored though she be, will be recognized as Lord Talbot's heiress. You have foreseen that too. You are a handsome young cavalier; you have won her love; she has given herself to you; at the worst, you can marry her. Don't deprecate your scheme, my lord; I consider it sublime. If I were not myself, I would like to be you.

FABIANI.

Thank you.

THE MAN.

You have managed the matter very skillfully. You have concealed your name. You are safe as far as the Queen is concerned. The poor girl thinks she has been seduced by a nobleman from Somerset county, named Amyas Pawlet.

FABIANI.

All—he knows it all! Well, come to the point. What do you want of me?

THE MAN.

My lord, suppose some one had in his possession the papers which prove the birth, existence, and rights of Talbot's heiress! It would make you as poor as my ancestor Job, Don Fabiano, and would leave you no better castles than your castles in Spain, which would be very hard for you.

FABIANI.

Yes! But no one has those papers.

THE MAN.

Yes. Some one has them.

FABIANI.

Who?

THE MAN.

I.

FABIANI.

You, miserable wretch! It isn't true! Jew speaks, Jew lies.

THE MAN.

I have got the papers.

FABIANI.

You lie! Where have you got them?

THE MAN.

In my pocket.

FABIANI.

I don't believe you. Are they all in order? Nothing lacking?

THE MAN.

Nothing is lacking.

FABIANI.

Then I must have them.

THE MAN.

Gently.

FABIANI.

Jew, give me those papers!

THE MAN.

Excellent! Jew, miserable beggar who crawls through the streets, give me the city of Shrewsbury, give me the city of Wexford, give me the earldom of Waterford! Charity, if you please!

FABIANI.

Those papers are everything to me and nothing to you.

THE MAN.

Simon Renard and Lord Chandos would pay me pretty high for them.

FABIANI.

Simon Renard and Lord Chandos are two dogs between whom I will have you hanged.

THE MAN.

You have nothing else to say to me? Then farewell.

FABIANI.

Come back! What do you want me to give you for those papers?

THE MAN.

Something which you have with you.

FABIANI.

My purse?

THE MAN.

Out upon you! Do you want mine?

FABIANI.

What then?

THE MAN.

There is a parchment which never leaves you. It is a signature in blank which the Queen gave you, and in which she swears, upon her Catholic crown, to grant any favor he may ask, to the one who presents it. Give me that signature in blank, and you shall have Jane Talbot's titles. Paper for paper.

FABIANI.

What do you want to do with this signature in blank?

THE MAN.

I will explain. Cards on the table, my lord. I have told you your affairs; now I will tell you mine. I am one of the principal money-dealers in Kantersten Street, Brussels. I lend money; it is my business. I lend ten and get back fifteen. I lend to every one: I would lend to the devil; I would lend to the Pope. Two months ago one of my creditors died, without paying me. It was an old exiled servant of the Talbot family. The poor man left nothing but a few rags: I seized them. Among these rags I found a box, and in the box some papers—Jane Talbot's papers, my lord, giving her entire history in detail and furnishing proofs for better times. The Queen of England had just given you Jane Talbot's estates. I was in great need of the Queen of England at that time, for I wanted to make a loan of ten thousand gold marks. I realized that I might do business with you. I came to England in this disguise; I made myself a spy upon you, upon Jane Talbot. I did it all myself. In this way I learned everything, and here I am. You shall have Jane Talbot's papers if you give me the Queen's signature in blank. I will write upon it that the Queen shall give me ten thousand gold marks. They owe me something at the excise-office, but I won't haggle. Ten thousand gold marks—nothing more. I don't ask you for the sum, because only a crowned head could pay it. I am speaking frankly, you see. Two men as clever as we are, my lord, have nothing to gain by deceiving each other. If frankness were banished from the earth, it would be re-discovered in a *tête-à-tête* between two rogues.

FABIANI.

Impossible! I can't give you this signature in blank. Ten thousand gold marks! What would the Queen say? And then, to-morrow I may be disgraced: this signature in blank is my safeguard. This signature in blank is my head.

THE MAN.

What does that matter to me?

FABIANI.

Ask me for something else.

THE MAN.

I want that.

FABIANI.

Jew, give me Jane Talbot's papers.

THE MAN.

My lord, give me the Queen's signature in blank.

FABIANI.

Accursed Jew, I will have to yield. [*Draws a paper from his pocket.*

THE MAN.

Show me the Queen's signature in blank.

FABIANI.

Show me Talbot's papers.

THE MAN.

Afterward.

[*They go close to the lantern.* Fabiani *stands behind the Jew, and with his left hand holds the paper under the Jew's eyes; he examines it. The Man reads.*

"We, Mary, Queen—" It is well. You see, my lord, I am like you. I have calculated upon everything. I have foreseen everything.

FABIANI (*draws a dagger with his right hand and plunges it into the Jew's throat*).

Except this!

THE MAN.

Oh, traitor! Help!

[*He falls. In falling he throws a sealed packet into the darkness behind him;* Fabiani *does not perceive it.*

FABIANI (*leaning over the body*).

Faith! I believe he is dead. Quick, the papers. [*He searches the Jew.*] What! he hasn't got them. He has nothing—nothing at all about him! Not a paper! He was lying, the old wretch! He deceived me: he wanted to rob me. Is it possible, you accursed Jew! No, he has nothing. That is clear. I have killed him for nothing. They are all alike, these Jews. To lie and steal, that is all they can do. Come, let us get rid of this corpse; I can't leave it here at the door. [*Goes up stage.*] I will see if the boatman is still there; he can help me throw it into the Thames.

[*He descends, and disappears behind the parapet.*

GILBERT (*enters from the opposite side*).

I thought I heard a cry!

[*He perceives the body stretched upon the ground under the lantern.*

Some one has been assassinated! The beggar!

THE MAN (*lifting himself half-way up*).

Ah, you come too late, Gilbert.

[*He points to the place where he threw the packet.*

Take them. They are the papers which prove that Jane, your betrothed, is daughter and heiress of the last Lord Talbot. My assassin is Lord Clanbrassil, the Queen's favorite. Oh, I suffocate! Gilbert, avenge me! Avenge yourself! [*He dies.*

GILBERT.

Dead! Avenge myself? What does he mean? Jane, daughter to Lord Talbot? Lord Clanbrassil! The Queen's favorite? Oh, I am lost in wonder! [*Shaking the body.*] Speak! One word more! He is indeed dead!

SCENE VII

GILBERT, FABIANI

FABIANI (*returning*).

Who goes there?

GILBERT.

A man has been assassinated.

FABIANI.

No, a Jew.

GILBERT.

Who killed him?

FABIANI.

Faith! You or I.

GILBERT.

Sir?

FABIANI.

No witnesses. A corpse on the ground. Two men beside it. Which is the assassin? There is nothing to prove it is one rather than the other—I rather than you.

GILBERT.

Miserable man! You are the assassin!

FABIANI.

Well, yes! To be frank, I am. What of it?

GILBERT.

I am going to call the constables.

FABIANI.

You are going to help me throw the body into the water.

GILBERT.

I will have you seized and punished.

FABIANI.

You will help me throw the body into the water.

GILBERT.

You are insolent.

FABIANI.

Do as I say! Let us destroy all traces of this. Believe me, you are more interested in the matter than I am.

GILBERT.

Upon my soul!

FABIANI.

One of us two did the deed. I am a great lord, a nobleman. You are a passer-by, a peasant, a man of the people. A noble who kills a Jew pays a fine of four sous; a man of the people who kills one of his fellow-creatures is hanged.

GILBERT.

You would dare—

FABIANI.

If you denounce me, I will denounce you. I will be believed sooner than you. At any rate, the chances are unequal. Four sous fine for me, and the gallows for you.

GILBERT.

No witnesses! No proofs! Oh, my brain is bewildered! This miserable man is right, he has me in his power.

FABIANI.

Shall I help you throw the corpse into the river?

GILBERT.

You are a demon!

[Gilbert *takes the body up by the head,* Fabiani *by the feet; they carry it to the parapet.*

FABIANI.

Yes. Faith, my friend, I can no longer exactly tell which of us killed this man!

[*They go down behind the parapet.* Fabiani *re-appears.*

It is done. Good-night, comrade! Go your way!

[*He starts toward the house, but turns back, seeing that* Gilbert *follows him.*

Well, what do you want? Money for your trouble? In truth, I don't owe you anything, but here, take this.

[*He gives his purse to Gilbert, whose first impulse is to refuse it, but who accepts it afterward with the air of a man who has reflected.*]

Well, go! What more are you waiting for?

GILBERT.

Nothing.

FABIANI.

Then stay, if it pleases you. You can have the fine starlight while I have the pretty girl. God be with you!

[*He starts toward the door of the house and is about to open it.*]

GILBERT.

Where are you going?

FABIANI.

Faith, into my house!

GILBERT.

How? Into your house!

FABIANI.

That is what I said.

GILBERT.

Which of us two is dreaming? A short time ago you told me that I was the Jew's assassin! Now you tell me that that house is yours.

FABIANI.

Or that of my mistress, which amounts to the same thing.

GILBERT.

Repeat what you have just said.

FABIANI.

My friend, I say, since you wish to know, that this house

belongs to a beautiful girl named Jane, who is my mistress.

GILBERT.

And I tell you, my lord, that you lie! I tell you that you are a liar and an assassin! I tell you that you are an insolent knave! I tell you, you have pronounced some fatal words which will kill us both—you, for having said them: me, for having heard them.

FABIANI.

Dear me! Who the devil is this man?

GILBERT.

I am Gilbert the engraver. Jane is my betrothed.

FABIANI.

And I am the Chevalier Amyas Pawlet. Jane is my mistress.

GILBERT.

You lie, I tell you! You are Lord Clanbrassil, the Queen's favorite. Don't you think I know that, fool!

FABIANI (*aside*).

Everybody seems to know me to-night. Another dangerous man, whom we must get rid of.

GILBERT.

Tell me instantly that you have lied like a coward, and that Jane is not your mistress!

FABIANI.

Do you know her writing?

[*He takes a note from his pocket.*

Read this!

[*Aside, while* Gilbert *tremblingly unfolds the paper.*

If he would go in and quarrel with Jane, it would give my people time to get here.

GILBERT (*reading*).

"I will be alone to-night. You can come." Malediction! My lord, you have dishonored my betrothed, you are an infamous wretch! I demand my revenge.

FABIANI (*putting his hand to his sword*).

Willingly! Where is your sword?

GILBERT.

Oh, fury! To be one of the people! To have nothing—neither sword nor dagger. Well, you can go; but I will wait for you at night, in a corner of the street, and I will stick my nails into your throat, and I will assassinate you, you villain!

FABIANI.

Dear me! How violent you are, my friend.

GILBERT.

I will be revenged upon you, my lord!

FABIANI.

You! Revenged upon me? You so low, upon me so high! You are crazy! I defy you.

GILBERT.

You defy me?

FABIANI.

Yes.

GILBERT.

You shall see.

FABIANI (*aside*).

To-morrow's sun must not rise for this man. [*Aloud.*] Friend, listen to me. Go into your house. I am sorry you found it out, but I leave the beauty to you. Go in.

[*He throws a key down at* Gilbert's *feet.*

There is a key, if you haven't got one. Or, if you like it better, you can knock against the shutter three times and Jane will think it is I, and let you in. Good-night. [*He goes off.*

SCENE VIII

GILBERT (*alone*).

He is gone. He is no longer here. I did not grind and crush him beneath my feet. I had to let him go. Not a weapon about me.

[*He sees on the ground the dagger with which* Lord Clanbrassil *killed the Jew; he picks it up with fearful haste.*

Ah, you come too late; you can probably kill no one but myself. All the same, whether you fall from heaven or are vomited up from hell, I bless you. My Jane has betrayed me! Jane has given herself to this infamous man. Jane is the heiress of Lord Talbot. Jane is lost to me! O God! more terrible things have come to me in this hour than my brain can stand.

[Simon Renard *appears in the darkness at the back.*

Oh, to be revenged on that man! To be revenged on this Lord Clanbrassil! If I go to the Queen's palace, the lackeys will kick me out as if I were a dog. I am mad! My head will burst! I am willing to die, but I want to be revenged. I would give my blood for revenge! Will nobody in the world make this bargain with me? Who will give me vengeance on Lord Clanbrassil and take my life in payment?

SCENE IX

Gilbert, Simon Renard

SIMON RENARD (*taking a step forward*).

I will.

GILBERT.

You? Who are you?

SIMON RENARD.

The man you want.

GILBERT.

Do you know who I am?

SIMON RENARD.

You are the man I need.

GILBERT.

There is no longer but one thought in my mind, do you know that? To be revenged on Lord Clanbrassil and to die!

SIMON RENARD.

You shall be revenged on Lord Clanbrassil and you shall die.

GILBERT.

Who ever you may be, I thank you.

SIMON RENARD.

Yes, you shall have the vengeance you desire. But do not forget upon what condition. I must have your life.

GILBERT.

Take it.

SIMON RENARD.

It is agreed?

GILBERT.

Yes.

SIMON RENARD.

Follow me!

GILBERT.

Where?

SIMON RENARD.

You shall know.

GILBERT.

Remember that you have promised to avenge me!

SIMON RENARD.

Remember that you have promised to die.

SECOND DAY

THE QUEEN

SCENE.—*A room in the royal apartment. The gospel open on a prie-Dieu. The royal crown upon a stool. Side doors. A large door in the center. A portion of the background concealed by a large tapestry, representing a grand tournament*

SCENE I

THE QUEEN, *splendidly dressed, reclining upon a couch;*
FABIANO FABIANI *seated on a folding-chair. Magnificent
costume. The garter*

FABIANI *(a guitar in his hands, singing).*

> When you sleep, calm and pure, love,
> In shadow, 'neath my eyes,
> And your soft breathing gives my heart
> Its tenderest replies;
> On your sweet form my eyes can feast,
> Oh, beauty's priceless store!
> Then sleep, my beauty, sleep, my love,
> Sleep on, for evermore!
>
> And when you say, "I love you,"
> In truth, it seems to be
> As if God's heaven were opening
> Especially for me.
> I see dreams hidden in your eyes
> That we've not dreamed before;
> Then love me, oh, my beauty,
> Love me for evermore!
>
> You see, the whole of life, dear,
> Lies in those words, just four—
> All things that people envy,

All things that men adore,
All things that are seductive
On which our hearts set store,
To sing, to laugh, my beauty,
To sleep, to love, no more!

[*He puts down his guitar.*

Oh, I love you more than I can tell, madame! But this Simon Renard—this Simon Renard, who is more powerful here than you yourself—I hate him!

THE QUEEN.

I can't help it, my lord; you know that. He is here as the ambassador of the Prince of Spain, my future husband.

FABIANI.

Your future husband!

THE QUEEN.

Come, my lord, let us not speak of that. I love you! What more do you wish? Moreover, it is time for you to go, now.

FABIANI.

One moment more, Mary!

THE QUEEN.

It is time for the secret council to meet. Until now, there has been only a woman here. We must let the Queen enter.

FABIANI.

I wish the woman would keep the Queen waiting at the door.

THE QUEEN.

You wish, do you? You wish, do you? Look at me, my lord! Fabiani, you have a young and beautiful head!

FABIANI.

It is you who are beautiful, madame. You need only your

beauty to be all-powerful. There is something on your head which tells me you are the Queen; but it is written plainer on your brow than on your crown!

THE QUEEN.

Flatterer!

FABIANI.

I love you!

THE QUEEN.

You love me, do you not? You love only me? Say it to me again, just like that, with the same eyes! Alas! we poor women, we never know just what is passing in a man's heart. We have to trust your eyes; and the handsomest eyes, Fabiani, are often the most false. But yours, my lord, are so full of loyalty, so full of candor, so full of good faith, they could not deceive, those eyes—could they? Yes, my beautiful page, your glances are artless and sincere. Oh, it would be shameful to take such heavenly eyes to betray with! Your eyes are the eyes either of a devil or an angel!

FABIANI.

Neither angel nor devil. A man who loves you!

THE QUEEN.

Who loves the Queen?

FABIANI.

Who loves Mary.

THE QUEEN.

Listen to me, Fabiani. I love you, too. You are young; there are many beautiful women who smile tenderly on you—I know it. People get tired of queens as well as of other women.—Don't interrupt me!—If you ever fall in love with another woman, I want you to tell me about it.—Don't interrupt me, dear!—I may forgive you, if you tell me about it. You don't know how much I love you. I don't know myself. It is true, there are moments when I would rather see you dead than happy with another; but there are also moments when I would rather have you happy. Indeed, I don't know why they try to make me out such a wicked woman!

FABIANI.

I can only be happy with you, Mary! I love no one but you!

THE QUEEN.

Are you sure? Look at me! Are you sure? Oh, I am jealous sometimes! I imagine—where is the woman who does not think of these things?—sometimes I imagine that you are false to me. I would like to be invisible, so that I might follow you, and always know what you are doing, what you are saying, where you are! In fairy stories they tell about a ring which makes one invisible; I would give my crown to have such a ring as that. I keep thinking that you go to see the beautiful women in the city. Oh, you must not deceive me—indeed, you must not!

FABIANI.

Banish such thoughts from your mind, madame. I false to you, my love, my queen, my kind mistress! To do that, I would have to be the most thankless, the most miserable of men. And I have given you no reason to think me the most thankless, the most miserable of men. I love you, Mary; I adore you! I could not even look at another woman! I love you, I say; but don't you see it in my eyes? There must be some way to persuade you! Look at me well! Do I look like a man who is false? When a man deceives a woman, you can see it at once. Women are seldom mistaken about that.

And what a time you choose to tell me these things—the one moment in my life when I love you the most! It is true, I am sure I never loved you so much as I do to-day. I am not speaking to the Queen. What do I care about the Queen? What can she do to me? She can have my head cut off; what does that amount to? You, Mary, can break my heart. It isn't your sovereignty that I love, it is yourself. It is your beautiful white and soft hand that I love to kiss; it isn't your scepter, madame.

THE QUEEN.
Thank you, my Fabiano. Good-by! Ah, my lord, how young you are! What beautiful black hair, what a graceful head you have! Come back to me in an hour.

FABIANI.
What you call an hour, I call a century!

[*He goes out. As soon as he is gone,* The Queen *rises hastily, goes to a concealed door, opens it, and ushers in* Simon Renard.

SCENE II

The Queen, Simon Renard

THE QUEEN.
Come in, Sir Bailiff! Well, did you stay there? Did you hear him?

SIMON RENARD.
Yes, madame.

THE QUEEN.

What do you say to it? Oh, of all men on earth he is the most false, the most deceitful! What do you say to it?

SIMON RENARD.

I say, madame, that it is plain to be seen his name ends in *i*.

THE QUEEN.

Are you sure that he goes to this woman at night? Did you see him?

SIMON RENARD.

I myself, Chandos, Clinton, Montague. Ten witnesses!

THE QUEEN.

Oh, it is indeed infamous!

SIMON RENARD.

The whole affair will be still better proved to the Queen in a short time. The young woman is here, as I told your Majesty. I had her brought from her house last night.

THE QUEEN.

Isn't this a sufficient crime for his execution, sir?

SIMON RENARD.

What! To go to see a pretty girl by night! Oh, no, madame! Your Majesty had Frogmorton tried for a similar crime. Frogmorton was acquitted.

THE QUEEN.

I punished Frogmorton's judges.

SIMON RENARD.

Try not to have to punish Fabiani's judges.

THE QUEEN.

How shall I revenge myself on this traitor?

SIMON RENARD.

Your Majesty wants only a certain kind of revenge?

THE QUEEN.

The only kind worthy of me!

SIMON RENARD.

Frogmorton was acquitted, madame. There is only one way. I have explained it to your Majesty. The man who is there!

THE QUEEN.

Will he do whatever I wish?

SIMON RENARD.

If you do all that he wishes.

THE QUEEN.

Will he give his life?

SIMON RENARD.

He will make his own conditions, but he will give his life.

THE QUEEN.

What does he want? Do you know?

SIMON RENARD.

What you yourself want—revenge!

THE QUEEN.

Bid him come in, but stay you out there, within call, Sir Bailiff.

SIMON RENARD (*coming back*).

Madame!

THE QUEEN.

Tell my Lord Chandos to hold himself in the next room, with six men of my ordinance, in readiness to appear. And the woman also, let her be ready to appear. Go.

[Simon Renard *goes out.*

Oh! it would be frightful!

[The Queen *alone. A side door opens;* Simon Renard *and* Gilbert *enter.*

SCENE III

THE QUEEN, GILBERT, SIMON RENARD

GILBERT.
Before whom do I stand?
SIMON RENARD.
Before the Queen.
GILBERT.
The Queen!
THE QUEEN.
Yes, the Queen. I am the Queen. There is no time for astonishment. You, sir, are Gilbert, a workman, an engraver. You live somewhere beyond the borders of the river, with a woman named Jane, who is your betrothed, and who deceives you, whose lover is a man named Fabiano, who deceives me. You want revenge, so do I. In order to get it, I must be able to make any disposition I please of your life. It is necessary that you should say what I command you to say, no matter what it is. For you, there must be no longer either false or true, good or bad, justice or injustice—nothing but my vengeance and my will. I shall require you to let me act, and to let yourself be acted upon. Do you consent?
GILBERT.
Madame—
THE QUEEN.
You shall have your revenge; but I warn you, it will cost you your life—that is all. Make your conditions. If you have an old mother and you want her tablecloth covered with ingots

of gold, speak, I will do it. Sell me your life as dear as you please.

GILBERT.

I am no longer willing to die, madame.

THE QUEEN.

What!

GILBERT.

I have been thinking about it all night. Nothing is proved yet. I saw a man who boasted that he was Jane's lover. How do I know that he did not lie? I saw a key! How do I know that he did not steal it? I saw a letter! How do I know that she was not forced to write it? I don't even know whether it was her writing; it was dark, I was excited, I could not see. I can't give up my life, which is her life, like that. I don't believe any of it, I am not sure of any of it, I have not seen Jane!

THE QUEEN.

It is easy to see that you love. You are like me, you refuse all the proofs. But if you see her, your Jane, if you hear her confess the crime, will you do what I wish?

GILBERT.

Yes, upon one condition.

THE QUEEN.

Tell it to me afterward. [*To* Simon Renard.] Bring this woman here at once.

[Simon Renard *goes out. The* Queen *places* Gilbert *behind a curtain which covers part of the background of the apartment.* Stand there!

[Jane *enters, pale and trembling.*

SCENE IV

The Queen; Jane; Gilbert *behind the curtain*

THE QUEEN.

Approach, young woman. You know who we are?

JANE.

Yes, madame.

THE QUEEN.

You know who is the man who seduced you?

JANE.

Yes, madame.

THE QUEEN.

He deceived you. He passed himself off for a nobleman called Amyas Pawlet?

JANE.

Yes, madame.

THE QUEEN.

You know now that it is Fabiano Fabiani, Earl of Clanbrassil?

JANE.

Yes, madame.

THE QUEEN.

Last night, when they seized you in your house, you had given him a rendezvous, you were waiting for him?

JANE (*wringing her hands*).

Heavens, madame!

THE QUEEN.

Answer!

JANE (*with feeble voice*).

Yes.

THE QUEEN.

You understand that there is no more hope, neither for him nor for you?

JANE.

Nothing but death! That is a hope!

THE QUEEN.

Tell me all about it. Where did you meet this man first?

JANE.

The first time I saw him was— But what is the use? A poor wretched girl of the people, frivolous and vain, in love with jewels and fine clothes, a girl dazzled with the handsome looks of a great lord—that is all. I am seduced, I am dishonored, I am lost. There is nothing to add to that. My God, madame, don't you see that each word I speak is killing me?

THE QUEEN.

Enough.

JANE.

Your anger is terrible, I know it, madame. My head bends now beneath the punishment you have prepared for me.

THE QUEEN.

Punishment for you? Do you think I concern myself about you, simpleton? Who are you, wretched creature, that the Queen should concern herself about you? Oh, no! Fabiano is my affair. As for you, madame, some one else will look out for your punishment.

JANE.

Well, madame, whoever that one may be, whatever the punishment, I will endure all without a murmur. I will even thank you if you will listen to one prayer I am about to make. There is a man who took me in, an orphan from my birth, who adopted me, brought me up, nourished me, loved me, and who loves me still; a man of whom I am most unworthy, toward whom I have been most guilty, and yet whose image lies at the bottom of my heart, beloved, revered, sacred as is that of God; a man who now, while I am speaking to you, finds his home empty, deserted, robbed, who can't understand it, and who rends his garments in anguish. Well, madame, what I ask of your Majesty is that he may never understand, that I may disappear without his knowing what has become of me, what I have done, or what you have done with me. Alas, kind Heaven, I do not know how to make you understand, but you ought to feel that I have a friend in him—a noble, generous friend. Poor Gilbert! yes, it is true, he respects me and believes me pure, and I do not want him to hate me and despise me! Oh, you understand me, don't you, madame? That man's respect is a great deal more to me than my life. And then it will make him suffer so much—such a surprise! He won't believe it at first. No, he will not believe it. My God! Poor Gilbert. Oh, madame, have pity on him and on me! He has done you no harm! In the name of Heaven, keep him from knowing the awful truth! In the name of Heaven, don't let him know that I am guilty. He will kill himself. Don't let him know that I am dead. He will die too.

THE QUEEN.

The man you are speaking of is here; he is listening to you; he will judge you, he will punish you! [Gilbert *appears.*

JANE.

Heavens! Gilbert!

GILBERT (*to the* Queen).

My life belongs to you, madame.

THE QUEEN.

Good. Have you any conditions to make?

GILBERT.

Yes, madame!

THE QUEEN.

What are they? We give you our royal word that we will grant them.

GILBERT.

This, madame. It is very simple. It is a debt of gratitude I pay to one of your noble lords, who employed me a great deal in my capacity as engraver.

THE QUEEN.

Speak!

GILBERT.

This lord has a secret liaison with a woman whom he cannot marry because she belongs to a proscribed family. This woman, who up to the present time has lived in concealment, is the only daughter and heiress of the last Lord Talbot, beheaded under King Henry VIII.

THE QUEEN.

What? Are you sure of what you are saying? You say, John Talbot, the good Catholic lord, the loyal defender of my mother of Aragon, has left a daughter? Upon my crown, if that is true, this child is my daughter. And what John Talbot did for the mother of Mary of England, Mary of England will do for the daughter of John Talbot.

GILBERT.

Then, of course, it will be a pleasure to your Majesty to give back Lord Talbot's estates to his daughter?

THE QUEEN.

Yes, truly, and to take them away from Fabiano. But are there proofs that this heiress exists?

GILBERT.

There are!

THE QUEEN.

And if there are not, we will make them! We are not a queen for nothing!

GILBERT.

Your Majesty will give back to Lord Talbot's daughter the estates, lands, rank, coat-of-arms, and device of her father. Your Majesty will remove her from all proscription, and will guarantee that her life shall be safe. Your Majesty will marry her to this lord, who is the only man she can marry. Upon these conditions, madame, you can dispose of me, of my liberty, of my life, and of my will as you see fit.

THE QUEEN.

Good! I will do what you have asked.

GILBERT.

Your Majesty will do what I have asked? The Queen of England swears it to me, Gilbert the engraver, upon her crown which is here, and upon the open gospel which is there?

THE QUEEN.

Upon the royal crown which is here, and the divine gospel which is there, I swear it.

GILBERT.

The compact is concluded, madame. Have a tomb prepared for me and a nuptial bed prepared for the lovers. The lord I speak of is Fabiani, Earl of Clanbrassil. Talbot's heiress, behold her!

JANE.

What does he say?

THE QUEEN.

Am I dealing with a fool? What do you mean? Have a care, sir! You are bold to mock the Queen of England! In the royal chambers people should look to their words; there are times when the lips bring the head to the block!

GILBERT.

You have my head, madame; I have your oath.

THE QUEEN.

You do not mean to say you are speaking seriously? This Fabiano—this Jane! Come, come!

GILBERT.

This Jane is the daughter and the heiress of Lord Talbot.

THE QUEEN.

Bah! Nonsense! Delusion! Fancy! Have you got the proofs?

GILBERT.

Complete!

[*He takes a packet from his breast.*

Read these papers.

THE QUEEN.

Have I time to read your papers? Did I ask for your papers? What do your papers matter to me? If they prove anything, upon my soul, I will throw them into the fire and nothing will be left of them.

GILBERT.

Nothing but your oath, madame!

THE QUEEN.

My oath, my oath!

GILBERT.

Upon the crown and upon the gospel, madame; that is to say, on your head and your soul—on your life in this world, and on your life in the next.

THE QUEEN.

But what do you want? Oh, I swear you are mad!

GILBERT.

What do I want? Jane has lost her rank, give it back to her! Jane has lost her honor, give it back to her! Proclaim her the daughter of Lord Talbot and the wife of Lord Clanbrassil, and then take my life.

THE QUEEN.

Your life! What do you want me to do with your life then? I didn't want it except to use for vengeance on this man—this Fabiano. You can't understand anything at all, can you? Well! I can't understand you, either. You talked about vengeance! That is the way you avenge yourself, is it? These men of the people are stupid! And after all, do you suppose I believe your ridiculous story about an heiress of Talbot? The papers! You show me papers! I won't look at them. Oh, a woman wrongs you, and you play the magnanimous. Well, do it if it suits you! I am not magnanimous! No! My heart is full of rage and hate. I will avenge myself and you shall help me! Oh, but this man is mad, mad, mad! My God! why do I need him? It is exasperating to have to deal with people like this, at such a serious time.

GILBERT.

I have your word, as Catholic Queen. Lord Clanbrassil has seduced Jane; he shall marry her!

THE QUEEN.

And if he refuses to marry her?

GILBERT.

You will force him to do it.

JANE.

Oh, no! Have pity upon me, Gilbert!

GILBERT.

Well, then, if this infamous wretch refuses, your Majesty can do what she pleases with him and with me!

THE QUEEN (*with joy*).

Ah, that is all I ask!

GILBERT.

In that case, I will do everything the Queen commands, provided the crown of the Countess of Waterford is solemnly replaced by the Queen on the sacred and inviolable head of Jane, who stands here!

THE QUEEN.

Everything?

GILBERT.

Everything! Even a crime, if it is a crime you want. I will not stop at treachery, which is more than a crime; nor at infamy, which is more than treachery.

THE QUEEN.

You will say what I want you to say? You will die the death that I want you to die?

GILBERT.

The death that you want me to die!

JANE.

Oh, my God!

THE QUEEN.

You swear it?

GILBERT.

I swear it!

THE QUEEN.

Then it is settled. It is enough! I have your word, you have mine! It is agreed.

[*She seems to reflect a moment.*

[*To* Jane.] You are not needed here: go out. I will send for you.

JANE.

Oh, Gilbert, what is this you have done? Oh, Gilbert, I am a wretched creature, and I don't dare to raise my eyes to you. Oh, Gilbert, you are more than an angel, for you have the virtues of an angel and a man's passions at the same time. [*She goes out.*

SCENE V

THE QUEEN, GILBERT, *afterward* SIMON RENARD, LORD CHANDOS, *and the Guards*

THE QUEEN (*to* Gilbert).

Have you a weapon about you? A knife, a dagger, anything!

GILBERT (*drawing from his breast* Lord Clanbrassil's *dagger*).

A dagger? Yes, madame.

THE QUEEN.

Good! Hold it in your hand!

[*She seizes his arm quickly.*

Sir bailiff D'Amont! Lord Chandos!

[*Enter* Simon Renard, Lord Chandos, *and Guards.*

Seize this man! He has threatened my life, with his dagger! I seized his arm as he was about to strike me. He is an assassin!

GILBERT.

Madame!

THE QUEEN (*low to* Gilbert).

Have you forgotten your agreement so soon? Is this the way you let me use you? [*Aloud.*] You are all witnesses that he had a dagger in his hand. Sir Bailiff, what is the name of the executioner of the Tower of London?

SIMON RENARD.

He is an Irishman called Mac Dermot.

THE QUEEN.

Send for him. I want to speak to him.

SIMON RENARD.

Yourself?

THE QUEEN.

Myself.

SIMON RENARD.

The Queen will speak to the executioner!

THE QUEEN.

Yes, the Queen will speak to the executioner. The head will speak to the hand! Send for him.

[*A Guard goes out.*

My Lord Chandos, and you, gentlemen, will answer to me for this man. Keep him there among you, back of you. Certain things are about to happen here which he must witness. Sir Lieutenant d'Amont, is Lord Clanbrassil in the palace?

SIMON RENARD.

He is there, in the painted chamber, awaiting the Queen's good pleasure to see him.

THE QUEEN.

Does he suspect anything?

SIMON RENARD.

Nothing.

THE QUEEN (*to* Lord Chandos).

Let him come in!

SIMON RENARD.

The entire Court is also waiting there. Will nobody be admitted before Lord Clanbrassil?

THE QUEEN.

Who are those among our nobles who hate Fabiani?

SIMON RENARD.

All!

THE QUEEN.

Which hate him the most?

SIMON RENARD.

Clinton, Montague, Somerset, Earl of Derby, Gerard Fitz-Gerard, Lord Paget, and the Lord Chancellor.

THE QUEEN (*to* Lord Chandos).

Admit them all—except the Lord Chancellor. Go! [Chandos *goes out.*

[*To* Simon Renard.] The worthy Bishop Chancellor is not any fonder of Fabiani than the rest, but he is a more scrupulous man.

[*Noticing the papers which* Gilbert *left upon the table.*

Ah, I must look over these papers!

[*While she is examining them, the door in the background*

opens. Those lords designated by The Queen *enter, making profound salutations.*

SCENE VI

The same. LORD CLINTON *and the other lords.*

THE QUEEN.

Good-day, gentlemen! God be with you, my lords! [*To* Lord Montague.] Anthony Brown, I do not forget that you held your own most worthily against John of Montmorency and the Count of Toulouse during my negotiations with my uncle, the Emperor! Lord Paget, to-day you will receive your letters patent of Baron Paget de Beaudesert in Stafford. And this is our old friend, Lord Clinton. We are always your good friend, my lord. It was you who exterminated Thomas Wyatt in St. James's Field. Let us all remember it, my lords. The crown of England was saved that day by a bridge which enabled my troops to reach the rebels, and by a wall which prevented the rebels from reaching me! The bridge was London Bridge. The wall was my Lord Clinton!

LORD CLINTON (*low to* Simon Renard).

The Queen has not spoken to me for six months. How kind she is to-day!

SIMON RENARD (*low to* Lord Clinton).

Patience, my lord. She will be kinder still, by-and-by.

THE QUEEN (*to* Lord Chandos).

My Lord Clanbrassil may enter. [*To* Simon Renard.] After he has been here a few moments—

[*She speaks to him in a low voice and indicates the door through which* Jane *passed.*

SIMON RENARD.

I understand, madame. [Fabiani *enters.*

SCENE VII

The same. FABIANI

THE QUEEN.

Ah, here he is!

[*She continues to speak to* Simon Renard *in a low voice.*

FABIANI (*everybody salutes him; he looks around him. Aside*).

What does this mean? There are only my enemies here, this morning! The Queen is speaking in a low tone to Simon Renard. The devil! She is laughing! It is a bad sign.

THE QUEEN (*graciously to* Fabiani).

God be with you, my lord!

FABIANI (*seizing her hand which he kisses*).

Madame— [*Aside.*] She smiled at me! The danger is not for me!

THE QUEEN (*still graciously*).

I want to speak to you.

[*She advances to the front of the stage with him.*

FABIANI.

And I also, I want to speak to you, madame. I have a right to reproach you! To keep me away, to exile me so long! Ah, it wouldn't be thus if you thought of me during these hours of absence as I think of you!

THE QUEEN.

You are unjust. Since you left me, I have thought of no one but you!

FABIANI.

Is that really true? Does so much happiness belong to me? Say it to me again!

THE QUEEN (*always smiling*).

I swear it to you!

FABIANI.

Then you do indeed love me as I love you?

THE QUEEN.

Yes, my lord! Truly, I have thought of no one but you. So much so, that I have tried to plan a pleasant surprise for your return.

FABIANI.

What do you mean? What surprise?

THE QUEEN.

A meeting which will give you pleasure!

FABIANI.

A meeting with whom?

THE QUEEN.

Guess! Can't you guess?

FABIANI.

No, madame!

THE QUEEN.

Turn around!

[*He turns and sees* Jane *on the threshold of the little door, which is half open.*

FABIANI (*aside*).

Jane!

JANE (*aside*).

It is he!

THE QUEEN (*with the same smile*).

My lord, do you know this young woman?

FABIANI.

No, madame!

THE QUEEN.

Young woman, do you know this lord?

JANE.

Truth before life! Yes, madame.

THE QUEEN.

So, my lord, you do not know this woman?

FABIANI.

Madame, this is a conspiracy. I am surrounded by enemies. This woman is doubtless in league with them. I do not know her, madame! I do not even know who she is, madame!

THE QUEEN (*rising and striking him in the face with her glove*).

Ah, you are a coward! You betray one and disown the other! You don't even know who she is? Do you want me to tell you? This woman is Jane Talbot, daughter of John Talbot, the good Catholic lord who perished on the scaffold for my mother. This woman is Jane Talbot, my cousin: Jane Talbot, Countess of Shrewsbury, Countess of Wexford, Countess of Waterford, peeress of England. That is who she is, this woman! Lord Paget, you are commissioner of the private seal; you will remember our words. The Queen of England solemnly recognizes this woman here present, as Jane, daughter and sole heiress of the last Earl of Waterford. [*Showing the papers.*] Here are the titles and the proofs, which you will have sealed with the great seal. It is our will.

[*To* Fabiani] Yes, Countess of Waterford, and it is proved! And you will give back her estates, you wretched man! Ah, you don't know this woman? You don't know who she is? Well, I am telling you! It is Jane Talbot. Shall I tell you more yet?
[*Looking him in the face, in a low voice, between her teeth.*
Coward, she is your mistress!
FABIANI.
Madame!
THE QUEEN.
That is what she is! Now, this is what you are! You are a man without soul, a man without heart, a man without brains. You are a liar and a villain! You are—By my faith, gentlemen, you need not draw away. I am quite willing you should hear what I have to say to this man. I am not lowering my voice, it seems to me. Fabiano, you are a wretch; a traitor to me, a coward to her; a lying lackey, the most vile, the lowest of all men. Yet it is true, I made you Earl of Clanbrassil, Baron of Dinasmonddy and what more? Baron of Darmouth in Devonshire. Ah, well! I was an idiot! My lords, I ask your pardon for having forced you to be elbowed by that man there. You, a knight! you, a noble! you, a lord! Compare yourself a little with those who are such. Look! look around you! There stand noblemen. There is Bridges, Baron Chandos; there is Seymour, Duke of Somerset. There are the Stanleys, who have been Earls of Derby since 1485. There are the Clintons, who have been barons since 1298. Do you imagine you are like these people—you? You say that you are allied to the Spanish family of Peñalver, but it is not true; you are only a bad Italian. Nothing—worse than nothing! Son of

a shoemaker in the village of Larino! Yes, gentlemen, the son of a shoemaker! I knew it, and I did not tell it; I concealed it, and I made believe I credited this man when he talked about his nobility. That is the way we are, we women. Oh, Heaven! I wish there were women here; it would be a lesson to them all. This scoundrel! this scoundrel! he betrays one woman and disowns the other. Infamous creature! Oh, yes, indeed you are infamous. What! I have been speaking all this time and he is not yet on his knees? On your knees, Fabiani! My lords, force this man to kneel!

FABIANI.

Your Majesty—

THE QUEEN.

This creature whom I have loaded with benefits! this Neapolitan lackey whom I have made a noble knight and a proud earl of England. Ah, I ought to have expected this! But I am always like that; I am obstinate, and afterward I see that I am wrong. It is my fault. Italian stands for liar: Neapolitan for coward. Every time that my father made use of an Italian, he repented of it. This Fabiani! You see Lady Jane, unfortunate child, to what a man you have surrendered yourself! But I will avenge you. Oh, I ought to have known it from the first. You will find nothing in an Italian's pocket but a stiletto, nothing in his soul but treachery.

FABIANI.

Madame, I swear to you—

THE QUEEN.

Good! Now he will perjure himself; he will descend to the depths of infamy; he will make us blush to our finger-tips before these men—we women who have loved him. He will not even lift up his head!

FABIANI.

Yes, madame, I will lift it up! I am lost; I see it clearly. My death is decided. You will make use of every means, dagger, poison—

THE QUEEN (*taking hold of both his hands and dragging him violently to the front of the stage*).

Poison! Dagger! What are you saying, Italian? A treacherous vengeance, a disgraceful vengeance—a vengeance from the back, a vengeance such as you take in your country? No, Signor Fabiani, neither dagger nor poison. Do I have to conceal myself? Do I have to hide in the corners of the street at night and make myself small when I want revenge? No, by my faith, I want the daylight! Do you hear, my lord?— the full noonday, the bright sun, the public square, the ax and the stake, the crowds in the street, the crowds at the windows, the crowds on the roofs! A hundred thousand witnesses! I want people to be afraid, do you hear, my lord? I want them to think it splendid, frightful, magnificent. I want them to say, "It is a woman who has been wronged, but it is a Queen who takes revenge!" This much envied favorite, this handsome, insolent young man, whom I have dressed in velvets and satins, I want to see him bent double, terrified and trembling, on his knees before a black cloth, with naked feet, with manacled wrists, hissed by the people, fingered by the executioner. On this white neck, where I have put a golden collar, I want to put a rope. I have seen how Fabiani looks upon a throne, I want to see how he looks upon a scaffold.

FABIANI.

Madame—

THE QUEEN.

Not a word! Not a word! You are indeed lost, as you say. You will mount the scaffold as did Suffolk and Northumberland. This will be a festival such as I have given before to my good city of London. You know how she hates you, this good city of mine! Faith, when one wants vengeance, it's a good thing to be Mary, Queen of England, daughter of Henry VIII. and mistress of four seas. When you are on the scaffold, you can make a long speech to the people, if you like, as Northumberland did, or a long prayer to God, as Suffolk did, in order to give pardon the time to arrive; but God is my witness that you are a traitor, and the pardon will not come. This wretched liar who talked of love to me, and this morning even said "thou" to me—Eh, gentlemen, it seems to amaze you that I talk thus openly before you; but I repeat it, what do I care?

[*To* Lord Somerset.] My lord duke, you are constable of the Tower; demand this man's sword!

FABIANI.

Here it is; but I protest. Admitting that it is proved that I deceived or seduced a woman—

THE QUEEN.

What does it matter to me whether you have seduced a woman? Do I concern myself about that? These gentlemen are witnesses, it is a matter of indifference to me!

FABIANI.

The seduction of a woman is not a capital offense, madame. Your Majesty could not procure Frogmorton's condemnation upon the same accusation!

THE QUEEN.

I believe he defies us now! The worm has become a serpent. Who says you are accused of that?

FABIANI.

Of what else am I accused? I am not an Englishman; I am no subject of your Majesty. I am a subject of the King of Naples and a vassal of the Holy Father. I will appeal to his embassador, the eminent Cardinal Polus, to save me. I will defend myself, madame. I am a stranger! I cannot be tried unless I have committed a crime—a real crime. What is my crime?

THE QUEEN.

You ask what your crime is?

FABIANI.

Yes, madame.

THE QUEEN.

You all hear this question that he has asked, my lords? You shall hear the answer. Listen, and look out for yourselves, all of you, however great you may be, because you will see that I need only stamp upon the earth with my foot to bring from out of it a scaffold. Chandos, open that folding-door. Call the Court—every one! Bid every one enter.

[*The door at the back is opened. The entire Court enters.*]

SCENE VIII

The same. THE LORD CHANCELLOR, *all the Court*

THE QUEEN.

Enter, enter, my lords! I am truly pleased to see you to-day. Good! good! The officers of the law this way: nearer, nearer! Where are the sergeants-at-arms of the House of Lords? Harriot and Herbert? Ah, there you are, gentlemen! Be welcome! Draw your swords. Good! Place yourselves at the right and at the left of that man. He is your prisoner.

FABIANI.

Madame, what is my crime?

THE QUEEN.

My Lord Gardiner, my learned friend, you are chancellor of England. We order you and the twelve lord commissioners of the Star Chamber, whom we regret not to see here, to assemble yourselves in haste. Strange things are passing in this palace. Listen, my lords! Madame Elizabeth has raised more than one enemy to our crown. We have had the Pietro Caro plot—that man who started the Exeter movement, and who communicated with Madame Elizabeth by means of a cipher cut on her guitar. We have had the treachery of Thomas Wyatt who roused the county of Kent. We have had the rebellion of the Duke of Suffolk, who was captured in the hollow of a tree, after his followers were defeated. To-day we have a new attempt. Listen, all of you. To-day, this morning, a man presented himself at my audience. After a few words, he drew his dagger on me. I stopped his hand in time. Lord Chandos and the bailiff D'Amont seized the man. He says that he was urged to the crime by Lord Clanbrassil.

FABIANI.

By me! It is not true! This is a frightful thing! This man does not exist. This man cannot be found! Who is he? Where is he?

THE QUEEN.

He is here!

GILBERT (*coming out from among the soldiers, behind whom he has been hidden up to this time*).

I am the man!

THE QUEEN.

According to this man's declarations, we Mary, Queen, accuse before the Star Chamber this other man, Fabiano Fabiani, Earl of Clanbrassil, of high treason, and of an attempt of regicide upon our imperial and sacred person.

FABIANI.

Regicide? I? This is monstrous. Oh, my brain is bewildered! I cannot see clear! What is this trap? Whoever you may be, wretched creature, dare you affirm that what the Queen says is true?

GILBERT.

Yes!

FABIANI.

I urged you to regicide?

GILBERT.

Yes.

FABIANI.

Yes, always yes! Malediction! Oh, it is impossible for you to know how false that is, gentlemen. That man comes from hell! Unfortunate wretch, you want to ruin me, but don't you see that you ruin yourself in the same breath? The crime you charge upon me falls upon you too. You will send me to the block, but you will die also. Madman, with a single word you cause two heads to fall! Did you know that?

GILBERT.

I know it.

FABIANI.

My lords, this man is bribed—

GILBERT.

By you. Here is the purse full of gold which you paid me for the crime. Your crest and your monogram are embroidered upon it.

FABIANI.

Just Heaven! But you don't show me the dagger with which this man, it is said, attempted to strike the Queen. Where is the dagger?

LORD CHANDOS.

Here it is!

GILBERT (*to* Fabiani).

It is yours. You gave it to me for that purpose. They will find the sheath at your house!

THE LORD CHANCELLOR.

Earl of Clanbrassil, what reply do you make? Do you recognize this man?

FABIANI.

No!

GILBERT.

In truth, he only saw me by night. Let me whisper two words to him, madame, they will help his memory. [*He approaches Fabiani.*] My lord, you appear to recognize no one to-day— neither the man you have wronged, nor the woman you have seduced. Ah, the Queen avenges herself; but the man of the people, he avenges himself also. You defied me to do it, I think. Behold yourself caught between a double vengeance, my lord! What do you say to that? I am Gilbert the engraver!

FABIANI.

Yes, I recognize you. My lords, I recognize this man. Since it is with him I have to deal, I have nothing more to say.

THE QUEEN.

He confesses!

THE LORD CHANCELLOR (*to* Gilbert).

According to Norman law and Statute 25, Henry VIII., in a case of high treason of the first degree, a confession does not save the accomplice. Do not forget, it is a case wherein the Queen has not the right of mercy, and you will die upon the scaffold as well as the man you accuse. Therefore reflect! Do you confirm all you have said?

GILBERT.

I know that I shall die, and I confirm it.

JANE (*aside*).

My God! if this is a dream, it is very horrible.

THE LORD CHANCELLOR (*to* Gilbert).

Are you willing to repeat your statements with your hand upon the gospel?

[*He presents the gospel to* Gilbert, *who puts his hand upon it.*

GILBERT.

With my hand upon the gospel, and my approaching death before my eyes, I swear that this man is an assassin; that this dagger, which is his, was used for the crime; that this purse, which is his, was given to me in payment for the crime. May God help me! It is the truth!

THE LORD CHANCELLOR (*to* Fabiani).

My lord, what have you to say?

FABIANI.

Nothing! I am lost.

SIMON RENARD (*low to* The Queen).

Your Majesty sent for the executioner. He is there!

THE QUEEN.

Good! Let him come in!

[*The row of noblemen divides and the Executioner appears; he is dressed in red and black, and on his shoulder bears a long sword in its scabbard.*

SCENE IX

The same. EXECUTIONER

THE QUEEN.

My lord Duke of Somerset, these two men to the Tower! My Lord Gardiner, our chancellor, let their trial before the twelve peers of the Star Chamber commence to-morrow, and may God keep watch over England. We expect them to be judged, both of them, before we leave for Exford, where we are to open Parliament, and for Windsor, where we are to spend Easter.

[*To the* Executioner.] Approach! I am glad to see you! You are a faithful servant. You are old; you have already witnessed three reigns. It is customary for the sovereigns of this kingdom to make you as costly a gift as possible, upon their ascension. My father, Henry VIII., gave you the diamond clasp of his cloak. My brother, Edward VI., gave you a goblet of chased gold. It is my turn now; I have not given you anything yet. I must give you a present. Come nearer! [*Indicating* Fabiani.] Do you see that head—that young, adorable head; that head, which, up to this morning, was the dearest, the most precious thing to me, in all my kingdom? Well! that head—look at it well—I give it to you!

THIRD DAY

PART I. WHICH OF THE TWO?

SCENE.—*Hall in the interior of the Tower of London. Pointed arch upheld by large pillars. To the right and to the left two low doors to two cells. To the right a dormer-window, which is supposed to overlook the Thames. To the left a dormer-window, which is supposed to overlook the streets. On each side a door concealed in the wall. In the background, a gallery with a sort of balcony shut in by glass and overlooking the exterior courts of the Tower*

SCENE I

GILBERT, JOSHUA

GILBERT.
Well?

JOSHUA.

Alas!

GILBERT.

No more hope?

JOSHUA.

No more hope. [Gilbert *goes to the window.*

You won't see anything from the window.

GILBERT.

You inquired, didn't you?

JOSHUA.

I am only too sure.

GILBERT.

It is for Fabiani?

JOSHUA.

It is for Fabiani.

GILBERT.

How fortunate that man is! Maledictions on me!

JOSHUA.

Poor Gilbert! Your turn will come! To-day, it is he; to-morrow it will be you!

GILBERT.

What do you say? We are not thinking of the same thing. What are you talking about?

JOSHUA.

About the scaffold which they are building.

GILBERT.

And I—I am speaking of Jane!

JOSHUA.

Of Jane?

GILBERT.

Yes, of Jane! Only of Jane. What does the rest matter to me? You have forgotten, have you? You don't remember that for one whole month, glued to the bars of my cell, from which I can look into the street, I have watched her, pale and sad, wandering around the base of this tower, which holds two men, Fabiani and me. You have forgotten all about my anguish, have you, and my doubts, my misgivings? For which of us does she come? Poor wretch, I ask myself this question day and night. I asked you, Joshua; and last night you promised to try to see her, and speak to her. Oh, tell me! Did you learn anything! Is it for me she comes, or is it for Fabiani?

JOSHUA.

I learned that Fabiani is certainly to be beheaded to-day, and you to-morrow, and from that moment I confess I lost my head, Gilbert. The scaffold drove Jane entirely out of my thoughts. Your death—

GILBERT.

My death! What do you mean by that word! My death is that Jane loves me no longer. From the day that I was no longer beloved, I was dead. Oh, yes! truly dead. Joshua, what has remained of me since that time won't be worth taking to-morrow. Oh, Joshua, you don't know, you can't understand what a man is when he loves. If any one had said to me, two months ago, "Jane, your Jane without reproach, your Jane so pure, your love, your pride, your lily, your treasure, Jane will give herself to another; will you take her then?" I should have said, "No, I will not have her! rather death a thousand times for her and for myself." And I should have crushed under my feet any one who had dared to speak to me like that. If I would take her?—To-day, you know, Jane is no longer the Jane without stain, whom I adored, the Jane whose brow I hardly dared touch with my lips. Jane has given herself to another—to a wretch! I know it—and—well, it's all the same to me. I love her! My heart is broken, but I love her! I would kiss the hem of her dress, and I would ask her pardon, if she would only take me. She might be in the gutter with those who belong there, and I would take her out, and I would hold her close to my heart, Joshua! Joshua, I would give, not a hundred years of life, since I no longer possess one day, but the eternity which will be mine to-morrow, just to see her smile at me once more—just once more before my death—and to have her say to me those dear words she used to say, "I love you." Joshua, Joshua, that is the way a man's heart is, when he loves. You think you would kill the woman who betrays you? No, you wouldn't kill her; you would lie at her feet afterward, the same as before, only you would be sad. You think I am weak? What should I have gained in killing Jane? Oh, my heart will burst with all these unbearable thoughts! If she only loved me now, what would it matter to me, what she has done? But she loves Fabiani! But she loves Fabiani! It is for Fabiani that she comes here! There is one thing that is sure, it is that I want to die. Have pity on me, Joshua!

JOSHUA.

Fabiani will die to-day.

GILBERT.

And I to-morrow.

JOSHUA.

God is above all.

GILBERT.

I will be revenged on him to-day. To-morrow, he will be revenged on me!

JOSHUA.

My brother, here is the second constable of the Tower, Master Eneas Dulverton. You must go in. I will see you again to-night.

GILBERT.

Oh, to die without being beloved! To have no one to weep for us! Jane! Jane! Jane!

[*Re-enters his cell.*]

JOSHUA.

Poor Gilbert! Good God! Who could have foretold that what has happened would happen?

[*Goes out. Enter* Simon Renard *and* Master Eneas.]

SCENE II

Simon Renard, Master Eneas Dulverton

SIMON RENARD.

As you say, it is very extraordinary. But what can you expect? The Queen is crazy. She doesn't know what she wants. You can't count upon anything. She is a woman. I would like to know what she is here for. Well! a woman's heart is a riddle of which King Francis I. wrote the solution on that pane of glass at Chambord—

"A woman's heart is most capricious;Who trusts her, finds life not propitious."

Listen to me, Master Eneas. We are old friends; we must get through with this thing to-day. Everything here depends upon you. If you are ordered—[*He whispers to Eneas*] be slow about it; let it fall through skillfully. Let me have two clear hours before me to-night, and what I want will be accomplished; to-morrow there will be no favorite. I shall be all-powerful, and you will be baronet and lieutenant of the Tower the day after. Do you understand?

MASTER ENEAS.

I understand.

SIMON RENARD.

Very well. Some one is coming. We must not be seen together. Go out that way. I am going to meet the Queen. [*They separate.*

SCENE III

A JAILER *enters with caution, then ushers in* LADY JANE.

THE JAILER.

You are where you wished to be, my lady. Here are the doors to the two cells. My recompense, now, if you please.

[Jane *unfastens her diamond bracelet and gives it to him.*

JANE.

There it is.

THE JAILER.
   Thanks. Don't compromise me.
   [*He goes out.*
JANE (*alone*).
   Kind Heaven! What shall I do? It is I who have destroyed him. I must be the one to save him! I can never do it, never! A woman can do nothing! The scaffold— The scaffold! Oh, it is horrible! Come, no more tears; let us have action! I never can do it! I never can do it! Have mercy on me, my God! I think some one is coming. Whose voice is that? I recognize it. It is the Queen's voice! Ah, all is lost!
   [*She hides behind a pillar. The Queen and Simon Renard enter.*

SCENE IV

The Queen; Simon Renard; Jane, *concealed*

THE QUEEN.
   Ah, the change surprises you? I am no longer myself? Well, what does that matter to me? It is the truth! I don't want him to die—now!
SIMON RENARD.
   Yet yesterday, your Majesty ordered the execution to take place to-day.
THE QUEEN.
   As I ordered the day before, that the execution should take place yesterday. As I ordered Sunday that the execution

should take place Monday. To-day I ordered the execution to take place to-morrow.

SIMON RENARD.

As a matter of fact, since the second Sunday in Advent, when the decision was pronounced in the Star Chamber, and the two criminals came back to the Tower preceded by the executioner with the ax turned toward them—and that was three weeks ago—every day since then your Majesty has put the matter off until to-morrow.

THE QUEEN.

Well, can't you understand what that means, sir? Must I explain everything, and must a woman be forced to show her naked heart to you, because she is a Queen—unfortunate woman that she is—and because you represent the Prince of Spain, her future husband? You don't understand, you men, that with a woman the heart has its chastity as well as the body. Well, then, yes—since you want to know, since you make believe that you don't understand anything—yes, every day I put off Fabiani's execution until to-morrow, because every morning my courage fails me when I think that the bell of the Tower of London will ring out his death-knell; because to think they are sharpening an ax for that man, breaks my heart; because it kills me to think they will nail a coffin over him; because I am a woman, because I am weak, because I am insane, because I love him yet, my God! There! have you got enough? Are you satisfied? Do you understand now? Oh, some day, my lord, I will have my revenge on you, for all these things you have made me tell you!

SIMON RENARD.

Yet it ought to be about time to get through with this Fabiani!

You expect to marry my royal master, the Prince of Spain, madame!

THE QUEEN.

If the Prince of Spain is not satisfied, let him say so; we will marry somebody else. Suitors are not lacking. The son of the King of the Romans, the Prince of Piedmont, the Infante of Portugal, Cardinal Polus, the King of Denmark, and Lord Courtenay are as good noblemen as he!

SIMON RENARD.

Lord Courtenay! Lord Courtenay!

THE QUEEN.

An English baron is worth a Spanish prince, my lord. Besides, Lord Courtenay is descended from the emperors of the East. Oh, get mad if you like!

SIMON RENARD.

Fabiani has made himself hated by every one in London who has got a heart.

THE QUEEN.

Except by me!

SIMON RENARD.

Peasants and lords are united against him, and if he is not executed this very day, as your Majesty has promised—

THE QUEEN.

Well!

SIMON RENARD.

There will be an uprising among the people.

THE QUEEN.

I've got my lansquenets.

SIMON RENARD.

There will be a conspiracy among the nobles.

THE QUEEN.

I have the executioner.

SIMON RENARD.

Your Majesty swore upon your mother's prayer-book that you would not pardon him.

THE QUEEN.

Here is a signature in blank which he has sent to me, in which I swear on my imperial crown that I will pardon him! My father's crown is worth as much as my mother's prayer-book. One oath destroys the other. But who says that I will pardon him?

SIMON RENARD.

He has boldly betrayed you, madame!

THE QUEEN.

What does that matter? All men are alike about that. I don't want him to die. Listen, my lord—I mean Sir Bailiff. Good God! you confuse my mind so much that I can't even tell whom I am talking to. Oh, I know all that you want to say to me! I know he is a vile, degraded, contemptible man. I know it as well as you, and I blush for it. But I love him! What do you want me to do about it? I would probably love a better man less. Moreover, who are you—all of you—great as you may be? Are you any better than he? You will tell me that he is a favorite, and the English nation detests favorites! Don't I know that you only want to overthrow him to put the Earl of Kildare—that fool, that Irishman—in his place, that he may have twenty heads a day cut off? What does that matter to you? Don't talk to me about your Prince of Spain; you make light enough of him. Don't talk to me about the anger of M. de Noailles, the French embassador! M. de Noailles is an idiot, and I will tell him so to his face. As for me, I am a woman; I want things, and then I don't want them. I am not made all in one piece. That man's life is necessary to my life. Oh, I beg of you, don't put on that air of virginal sincerity and good faith. I know all your intrigues. Between us two, you know as well as I that he didn't commit the crime for which he is condemned. Well, it is settled. I don't want Fabiani to die. Am I the mistress, or am I not? Come, Sir Bailiff, let us talk about something else, will you?

SIMON RENARD.

I withdraw, madame. All your nobles have spoken to you through my voice.

THE QUEEN.

What do I care for my nobles!

SIMON RENARD (*aside*).

Suppose we try the people!

[*He goes out with respectful salutation.*

THE QUEEN (*alone*).

He went out with a singular expression. That man is capable of arousing a rebellion. I must hurry off to the City Hall. What ho! Some one! [*Master Eneas and Joshua appear.*

SCENE V

The same, without SIMON RENARD. MASTER ENEAS, JOSHUA

THE QUEEN.

Is it you, Master Eneas? This man and you, you must attend

to it that the Earl of Clanbrassil makes his escape at once.
MASTER ENEAS.

Madame—

THE QUEEN.

Very well! I won't trust you; I remember you are one of his enemies. Are there none but enemies of the man I love, around me? I will wager that this turnkey, whom I don't even know, he hates him too.

JOSHUA.

You are right, madame.

THE QUEEN.

My God! My God! This Simon Renard is more a king than I am a queen! What! not one person to trust? No one to whom I can give power to plan his escape?

JANE (*coming out from behind the pillar*).

Yes, madame, I!

JOSHUA (*aside*).

Jane!

THE QUEEN.

You! Who are you? Ah, it is you, Jane Talbot. What are you doing here? Never mind, you are here! You have come to save Fabiani; thank you! I ought to hate you, Jane; I ought to be jealous of you. I have reason enough to be! But I'm not! I love you for loving him! In front of the scaffold there is no more jealousy—nothing but love! You are like me, you forgive him. I understand; men don't understand these things. Lady Jane, let us have it clearly understood. We are both of us miserable, are we not? We must save Fabiani! I have no one but you. I must let you do it! At least, I am sure, you will do it with all your heart. Take charge of it, gentlemen, both of you. Do everything that Lady Jane directs you to do, and upon your heads, you will be answerable for the execution of her orders. Embrace me, young woman!

JANE.

The Thames washes the base of the Tower on this side. I noticed a secret passage. A boat at that place, and the escape might be made by the Thames. It is the safest way.

MASTER ENEAS.

It will be impossible to get a boat there, before an hour.

JANE.

That is very long.

MASTER ENEAS.

It will soon pass! It will be dark, too. That will be better if her Majesty wishes to keep the escape secret.

THE QUEEN.

Perhaps you are right. In one hour then. I leave you, Lady Jane. I must go to the City Hall. Save Fabiani!

JANE.

Make yourself easy, madame!

[The Queen *goes out;* Jane *follows her with her eyes.*

JOSHUA (*front of stage*).

Gilbert was right; she loves Fabiani!

SCENE VI

The same, without THE QUEEN

JANE (*to* Master Eneas).

You have heard the Queen's commands. A boat, there, at the base of the Tower, the keys of the secret corridors, a cap, and a cloak.

MASTER ENEAS.

Impossible to get all that before night. In one hour, my lady.

JANE.

Very well! Go! Leave me with this man.

[Master Eneas *goes out.* Jane *follows him with her eyes.*

JOSHUA (*aside, at front stage*).

"This man!" It is very natural. One who has forgotten Gilbert will not remember Joshua.

[*He goes to* Fabiani's *cell and is about to open it.*

JANE.

What are you doing there?

JOSHUA.

Forestalling your wishes, my lady. I am opening this door.

JANE.

What door is that?

JOSHUA.

The door of my Lord Fabiani's cell.

JANE.

And that one?

JOSHUA.

It is the door to another man's cell.

JANE.

Who is he—that other?

JOSHUA.

Another who is condemned to death; some one whom you do not know—a workman named Gilbert.

JANE.

Open that door!

JOSHUA (*after having opened it*).

Gilbert!

SCENE VII

JANE, GILBERT, JOSHUA

GILBERT (*from the interior of his cell*).

What is wanted?

[*He appears on the threshold, sees Jane, leans trembling against the wall.*

Jane! Lady Jane Talbot!

JANE (*on her knees, without lifting her eyes to him*).

Gilbert, I have come to save you!

GILBERT.

Save me!

JANE.

Listen to me! Pity me! Do not crush me! I know all that you would say. It is all true; but don't say it to me. I must save you. Everything is ready. The escape is safe. Let yourself be saved by me, just as if I were anybody else. I don't ask any more. You need never recognize me again. You need never know who I am! Don't forgive me! Just let me save you. Will you?

GILBERT.

Thank you! It is useless. Why wish to save my life, Lady Jane, if you do not love me?

JANE (*with joy*).

Oh, Gilbert, is that what you ask me, truly? Gilbert, do you deign to think of what is passing in this poor girl's heart? Gilbert, is it possible that the love I have for you can interest you, can seem worth thinking about? Oh, I thought it was quite indifferent to you—that you despised me too much to wonder what I did with my heart. Gilbert, if you only knew how these words you have spoken make me feel! Oh, it is an unhoped-for gleam of sunshine in my dark night. Oh, listen to me! If I dared to draw near to you, if I dared to touch your garments, if I dared to take your hand in mine, if I dared once more to lift mine eyes to you and to Heaven, as I did once—do you know what I would say to you? On my knees, prostrate, weeping at your feet, with sobs on my lips and the joy of angels in my heart, I would say, "Gilbert, I love you!"

GILBERT (*taking her to his heart with rapture*).

You love me?

JANE.

Yes, I love you!

GILBERT.

You love me! My God! she loves me. It is indeed true! She has said it herself; her lips have spoken it. God in heaven!

JANE.

My Gilbert!

GILBERT.

You say all is prepared for my escape? Quick—let us hurry! Life! I want to live! Jane loves me! This roof descends on my head and crushes it. I want air! I suffocate here! Let us fly quickly. Let us go, Jane! I want to live! I want to live! I am beloved.

JANE.

Not yet. We must have a boat. We must wait until night. But be easy. You are saved. In less than an hour we will be outside. The Queen is at the City Hall and will not come back so soon as that. I am mistress here. I will explain it all to you.

GILBERT.

Wait an hour? That is long. Oh, I yearn to get back to life and happiness. Jane, Jane, you are there; I will live! You love me! I am come back from hell! Restrain me. I will do something mad. I will laugh, I will sing. Ah, you do love then?

JANE.

Yes, I love you! yes, I love you! And listen, Gilbert, believe me; this is the truth as though I were on my death-bed: I have never loved any one but you. Even in my fall, even in the midst of my sin, I loved you. Scarcely had I fallen into the arms of that demon who ruined me, when I wept for my angel.

GILBERT.

Forgotten! forgiven! Never speak of it again, Jane! What do I care for the past? Who could resist your voice, who would do other than I am doing? Yes, I pardon everything, my well-beloved child. The foundation of love is mercy and pardon, Jane; jealousy and despair burned the tears in my eyes, but I pardon you, but I thank you! You are the only truly bright thing in this world; at each word that you speak, I feel grief dies, and joy is born in my soul. Jane, lift your head, stand up straight before me there and look at me! I tell you that you are my child.

JANE.

Always generous! Gilbert, my well-beloved.

GILBERT.

I wish I were outside now: in our flight, far away: free, with you! Oh, this night, which will never come! The boat is not there. Jane, we will leave London at once, this night. We will leave England; we will go to Venice. Men of my trade make a great deal of money there. You will belong to me! Oh, my God! I am insane! I have forgotten the name you bear. It is too proud a one, Jane.

JANE.

What do you mean?

GILBERT.

Daughter of Lord Talbot.

JANE.

I know one prouder still.

GILBERT.

Which?

JANE.

Wife of the workman Gilbert.

GILBERT.

Jane!

JANE.

Oh, no! Don't think I ask so much as that. I know I am unworthy of that. I do not lift my eyes so high. I would never take such an advantage of your pardon. The poor engraver Gilbert shall make no mesalliance with the Countess of Waterford. No, I will follow you, I will love you, I will never leave you; I will lie all day at your feet, all night at your door. I will watch you work, I will help you, I will give you all you need. I will be to you something less than a sister, something more than a dog. And if you ever marry, Gilbert—because God will want you to find somebody, some pure woman, without stain and worthy of you—well, if you marry, and if your wife is good, if she will let me, I will be your wife's servant. If she won't have me, I will go off, far off, to die where I can. That is the only way I shall ever leave you. If you do not marry I will stay with you, always; I will be gentle and patient—oh, you shall see!—and if people think ill of me because I am with you—well, they can think what they please. I have no longer the right to blush, you see—I am only an unfortunate woman!

GILBERT (*falling at her feet*).

You are an angel! You are my wife!

JANE.

Your wife? Ah, you are like God—your pardon purifies me. Be blessed, Gilbert, for putting this crown upon my brow.

[Gilbert *takes her up and folds her to his heart. While they stand thus in each other's arms,* Joshua *takes* Jane's *hand.*

JOSHUA.

It is Joshua, Lady Jane!

JANE.

Good Joshua!

JOSHUA.

You did not know me a little while ago.

JANE.

No, I had to begin with him.

[Joshua *kisses her hand.*

GILBERT (*pressing her in his arms*).

Ah, what happiness! But is it real, all this happiness?

[*For some time a distant noise has been heard; confused voices, a tumult. It grows dark.*

JOSHUA.

What is that noise?

[*He goes to the window which overlooks the street.*

JANE.

Oh! My God! Let nothing happen!

JOSHUA.

There is a great crowd off there. Pick-axes, pikes, torches. The Queen's pensioners on horseback, and fighting. They are all coming this way! What cries! The devil! It looks like a public revolt.

JANE.

If it is only not against Gilbert.

DISTANT CRIES.

Fabiani! Death to Fabiani!

JANE.

Can you hear?

JOSHUA.

Yes.

JANE.

What are they saying?

JOSHUA.

I can't distinguish!

JANE.

Oh, my God! My God!

[*Master Eneas and a boatman enter hastily through the concealed door.*

SCENE VIII

The same. MASTER ENEAS, *a Boatman*

MASTER ENEAS.
My Lord Fabiani! My lord, not an instant to lose! The people know the Queen wanted to save your life. There is a revolt of the London populace against you. In a quarter of an hour you will be torn to pieces. My lord, save yourself. Here is a cloak and a cap. Here are the keys. Here is a boatman. Don't forget that you owe it all to me. My lord, make haste! [*Low to Boatman.*] Remember, you are not to hurry.

JANE (*hastily covers* Gilbert *with the cloak and cap; low to* Joshua).
Heaven! If this man will only not recognize him.

MASTER ENEAS (*looking into* Gilbert's *face*).
What! this is not Lord Clanbrassil. You are not fulfilling the Queen's orders, my lady. You are helping another to escape.

JANE.
All is lost! I ought to have foreseen this! Ah, sir, it is true! Have mercy—

MASTER ENEAS (*low to* Jane).
Silence! Go on! I have said nothing! I have seen nothing!

[*He goes up stage with an air of indifference.*

JANE.
What does he say? Ah, Providence befriends us. Everybody wants to save Gilbert.

JOSHUA.
No, my lady, everybody wants to destroy Fabiani.

[*During the entire scene the cries have increased outside.*

JANE.

We must hurry, Gilbert. Come quickly.

JOSHUA.

Let him go alone!

JANE.

Leave him!

JOSHUA.

Only for a moment. No woman in the boat, if you want it to arrive safe. It is too light yet; your dress is white. After the peril is over, you will find each other again. Come this way with me. Let him go that way.

JANE.

Joshua is right. Where will I find you, my Gilbert?

GILBERT.

Under the first arch of London Bridge.

JANE.

Good! Go quickly. The tumult increases. Oh, I wish you were safe away!

JOSHUA.

Here are the keys. There are twelve doors to open and shut between here and the water's edge. It will take you a good quarter of an hour.

JANE.

A quarter of an hour! Twelve doors! That is frightful.

GILBERT (*embracing her*).

Good-by, Jane! A few more moments of separation and we will rejoin each other for a life-time!

JANE.

For eternity. [*To the Boatman.*] Sir, I place him in your care!

MASTER ENEAS (*low to Boatman*).

For fear of accident, don't hurry.

[*Gilbert goes out with the Boatman.*

JOSHUA.

He is saved! Now for us! We must shut this cell.

[*He shuts the door of* Gilbert's *cell.*

All right! Come quickly; this way!

[*He goes out, with* Jane, *through the other concealed door.*

MASTER ENEAS (*alone*).

Fabiani remains in the trap. Now, there is a shrewd little woman whom Simon Renard would have paid a good deal for. How will the Queen take all this? Provided the consequences do not fall on my shoulders!

[*The Queen and* Simon Renard *enter with rapid steps. The tumult outside has steadily increased. It is night. Cries of death, torches, lights, sounds of moving masses; the click of arms, shots, the stamping of horses. Several noblemen with daggers in their hands accompany* The Queen. *Among them are the herald of England, Clarence, bearing the royal banner, and the herald of the Order of the Garter, Jarretiere, bearing the banner of that order.*

SCENE IX

The Queen, Simon Renard, Master Eneas, Lord Clinton, *the two heralds, lords, pages, etc.*

The Queen (*low to* Master Eneas).

Has Fabiani escaped?

MASTER ENEAS.

Not yet!

THE QUEEN.

Not yet! [*Giving him a terrible look.*

MASTER ENEAS (*aside*).

The devil!

THE PEOPLE (*outside*).

Death to Fabiani!

SIMON RENARD.

You must make your decision on the spot, madame. The people demand this man's death! The Tower is besieged. The revolt is formidable. Your nobles have been cut to pieces on London Bridge. Your Majesty's pensioners hold their own yet; but, just the same, your Majesty has been chased street by street, from the City Hall to the Tower of London. Madame Elizabeth's followers have joined the people. You can tell that by the venom of the mob. All this is serious. What does your Majesty command?

THE PEOPLE.

Fabiani! Death to Fabiani!

[*They grow louder, and come nearer.*

THE QUEEN.

Death to Fabiani! Do you hear that howling populace, my lords? You must throw a man out to them. The rabble is hungry!

SIMON RENARD.

What does your Majesty command?

THE QUEEN.

By heaven, my lords! it seems to me you all stand trembling

around me! Upon my soul! must a woman show you your duty as noblemen? To horse, my lords, to horse! Are you afraid of the rabble? Are swords afraid of clubs?

SIMON RENARD.

Don't let things go any further. Yield, madame, while there is yet time. You can yet say "the rabble"; in an hour you will have to say "the people"!

[*The cries increase, the noise comes nearer.*

THE QUEEN.

In an hour!

SIMON RENARD (*going to gallery and returning*).

In a quarter of an hour, madame. The first wall of the Tower is broken down. One more step, the mob will be here.

THE PEOPLE.

To the Tower! to the Tower! Fabiani! death to Fabiani!

THE QUEEN.

How right they are who call the people terrible! Fabiano!

SIMON RENARD.

Do you want to see him torn to pieces before your eyes?

THE QUEEN.

Do you know this is infamous, that not one of you stirs? In the name of Heaven, defend me, my lords!

LORD CLINTON.

You? yes, madame. Fabiano? no!

THE QUEEN.

Very well, I will tell you all then, so much the worse for you. Fabiano is innocent. Fabiano never committed the crime for which he was condemned. It was I, and this man here, and the engraver Gilbert. We did it all; we invented it all; we imagined it all. It was all a farce! Contradict me if you dare, Sir Bailiff! Now, gentlemen, will you defend him? He is innocent; I swear it. On my head, on my crown, on my God, on my mother's soul, he is innocent of the crime. It is as true as that you stand there, Lord Clinton! Defend him! Annihilate these wretches as you annihilated Tom Wyatt, my brave Clinton, my old friend, my good Robert! I swear to you that it is false that Fabiano tried to assassinate the Queen.

LORD CLINTON.

There is another Queen whom he tried to assassinate—England!

[*The cries continue outside.*

THE QUEEN.

The balcony! Open the balcony. I myself will prove to the people that he is not guilty.

SIMON RENARD.

Prove to the people that he is not Italian.

THE QUEEN.

When I think it is Simon Renard, one of Cardinal Granvelle's creatures, who dares to speak to me like this! Well, open that door! open that cell! Fabiano is there. I want to see him; I want to speak to him.

SIMON RENARD (*low*).

What are you doing? For his own sake, you needn't let everybody know where he is.

THE PEOPLE.

Death to Fabiani! Long live Elizabeth!

SIMON RENARD.

They cry long live Elizabeth, now!

THE QUEEN.

My God! My God!

SIMON RENARD.

Choose, madame [*with one hand he points to the cell*], this head to the people [*with the other hand he designates the crown which* the Queen *wears*] or that crown to Madame Elizabeth.

THE PEOPLE.

Death! Death! Fabiani! Elizabeth!

[*A stone breaks through a pane of glass near* The Queen.

SIMON RENARD.

Your Majesty is destroying herself without saving him! The second court is reached. What does the Queen command?

THE QUEEN.

You are all cowards, and Clinton is the worst of all. Ah, Clinton, I will remember this, my friend!

SIMON RENARD.

What does the Queen command?

THE QUEEN.

Oh, to be abandoned by all of you! to have confessed all without obtaining anything! What sort of creatures are these noblemen here? That populace is infamous! I would like to crush them under my feet. There are times then, when a queen is nothing but a woman? You will pay dear for this, gentlemen!

SIMON RENARD.

What does the Queen command?

THE QUEEN (*crushed*).

Whatever you will. Do what you like. You are an assassin. [*Aside.*] Oh, Fabiano!

SIMON RENARD.

Clarence! Jarretiere! Come here! Master Eneas, open the great balcony of the gallery.

[*The balcony in the back opens.* Simon Renard *steps out upon it,* Clarence *at his right,* Jarretiere *at his left. Immense tumult outside.*

THE PEOPLE.

Fabiani! Fabiani!

SIMON RENARD (*on the balcony, turned toward the people*).

In the Queen's name!

HERALDS.

In the Queen's name!

[*Profound silence outside.*

SIMON RENARD.

People, the Queen bids you know this: To-day, this very night, one hour after the curfew, Fabiano Fabiani, Earl of Clanbrassil, covered with a black veil from head to foot, bound with an iron gag, a yellow wax candle weighing three pounds in his hand, will be led, by torchlight, from the Tower of London, through Charing Cross, to the old Market-Place of the city, there to be publicly punished and beheaded, for the crimes of high treason and attempt of regicide on the imperial person of the Queen!

[*Immense applause outside.*

THE PEOPLE.

Long live the Queen! Death to Fabiani!

SIMON RENARD (*continuing*).

And, in order that no one in this city of London shall ignore it, this is what the Queen orders during the entire journey, which the criminal must make from the Tower of London to the old Market-Place: The great bell of the Tower shall toll; at the moment of the execution, three cannon-shots will be fired—the first, when he mounts the scaffold; the second, when he kneels upon the black cloth; the third, when his head falls. [*Applause.*]

THE PEOPLE.

Illuminate! Illuminate!

SIMON RENARD.

This night the Tower and the city of London will be illuminated with lights and torches, in sign of joy. I have spoken. [*Applause.*] God protect the old charter of England!

THE TWO HERALDS.

God protect the old charter of England.

THE PEOPLE.

Death to Fabiani! Long live Mary! Long live the Queen!

[*The balcony is closed.* Simon Renard *approaches* The Queen.

SIMON RENARD.

What I have just done will never be forgiven me by the Princess Elizabeth!

THE QUEEN.

Nor by Queen Mary. Leave me, sir.

[*She dismisses them all with a gesture.*

SIMON RENARD (*low to* Master Eneas).

Master Eneas, look to the execution!

MASTER ENEAS.

Count upon me!

[Simon Renard *goes out. As* Master Eneas *is about to go,* The Queen *rushes to him, seizes him by the arm and drags him violently to the front of the stage.*

SCENE X

The Queen, Master Eneas

THE PEOPLE (*outside*).
 Death to Fabiani! Fabiani! Fabiani!
THE QUEEN.
 Whose head is worth most at this moment, do you think—Fabiani's or yours?
MASTER ENEAS.
 Madame!
THE QUEEN.
 You are a traitor!
MASTER ENEAS.
 Madame! [*Aside.*] The devil!
THE QUEEN.
 No explanations! I swear by my mother, if Fabiano dies, you die!
MASTER ENEAS.
 But, madame—
THE QUEEN.
 Save Fabiano, and you save yourself—not otherwise!
THE PEOPLE.
 Death to Fabiani! Fabiani!
MASTER ENEAS.
 Save the Earl of Clanbrassil? But the people are out there! It is impossible! By what means?
THE QUEEN.
 Find some!

MASTER ENEAS.

What could I do?

THE QUEEN.

Do what you would for yourself.

MASTER ENEAS.

The people will keep armed until after the execution. To satisfy them, somebody must be beheaded!

THE QUEEN.

Anybody you please.

MASTER ENEAS.

Anybody I please? Wait, madame! The execution will be at night, by torchlight; the criminal covered with a black veil, gagged; the people kept a long way from the scaffold by the pike-men, the same as always. It is enough, if the people see a head fall. The thing is possible. If only the boatman is there yet! I told him not to hurry.

[*He goes to the window which overlooks the Thames.*]

There he is, but we're just in time!

[*He leans out of the window, a torch in his hand, waving his handkerchief, then he turns to* The Queen.]

All right! I will answer for Lord Fabiani, madame!

THE QUEEN.

On your head?

MASTER ENEAS.

On my head!

THIRD DAY

PART II

SCENE.—*A hall or room into which lead two staircases, one ascending and the other descending. The entrance to each of these staircases fills a portion of the back of the stage. The one which ascends ends at the frieze; the one which descends ends underneath—neither the beginning nor the end is visible*

The room is draped with black in a peculiar fashion. The wall on the right, the wall on the left, and the ceiling are covered with a black cloth on which is a large white cross; the background, which faces the spectator, with a white cloth and large black cross. These black and white draperies continue until they are lost to sight under the staircases. To the right and to the left, there is an altar draped with black and white, decorated as if for a funeral. Tall candles. No priests. A few funeral lamps, hanging here and there from the vaulted roof, light the room and the staircases feebly. What really lights the room is the great white cloth in the background, through which a reddish light shines as if there were a fiery furnace behind. The room is paved with tombstones. As the curtain rises, the motionless figure of THE QUEEN *is seen in black outline on this transparent cloth*

SCENE I

JANE, JOSHUA. *They enter cautiously through a little door behind the black draperies, which they push aside*

JANE.

Where are we, Joshua?

JOSHUA.

On the great landing of the staircase down which the criminals go to execution. It was draped in this way under Henry VIII.

JANE.

No way of getting out of the Tower?

JOSHUA.

The people are on guard at every exit. They want to be sure of getting their criminal this time. No one can go out before the execution.

JANE.

The proclamation they made from the balcony rings in my ears yet. This is a horrible thing, Joshua.

JOSHUA.

Oh, I've seen many such!

JANE.

If only Gilbert has been able to escape. Do you think he is safe, Joshua?

JOSHUA.

I am sure of it.

JANE.

You are sure of it, good Joshua?

JOSHUA.

The Tower wasn't surrounded on the waterside. Then, when he started, the riot wasn't as bad as it was afterward. It was a fine riot, if you but knew it.

JANE.

You are sure that he is safe?

JOSHUA.

And waiting for you under the first arch of London Bridge, where you will meet him before midnight.

JANE.

Heaven! He will be anxious too.

[*Seeing the shadow of* The Queen.

My God! what is that, Joshua?

JOSHUA (*low, taking her hand*).

Silence! It is the lioness, on the watch.

[*While* Jane *looks at this figure in horror, a distant voice, which seems to come from above, pronounces these words slowly and distinctly.*

VOICE.

The man, covered with a black veil, who follows me, is the very high and mighty Lord Fabiano Fabiani, Earl of Clanbrassil, Baron of Dinasmonddy, Baron of Darmouth in Devonshire, who is to be beheaded at the London Market-Place, for the crimes of regicide and high treason. God have mercy on his soul!

ANOTHER VOICE.

Pray for him!

JANE (*trembling*).

Joshua, do you hear?

JOSHUA.

Yes, I hear such things every day.

[*A funeral procession appears at the head of the staircase, and gradually forms itself on the steps as it descends. A man dressed in black is at the head, bearing a white banner with black cross. Next comes* Master Eneas Dulverton, *wearing a great black cloak, holding his Constable's baton in his hand. Then a group of halberdiers, dressed in red; then a man in white, bearing black banner with white cross. To the right and to the left, halberdiers bearing torches.*

JANE.

Do you see?

JOSHUA.

Yes, I see such things every day.

[*As they are about to reach the stage the procession stops.*

MASTER ENEAS.

The man, covered with a black veil, who follows me, is the very high and mighty Lord Fabiano Fabiani, Earl of Clanbrassil, Baron of Dinasmonddy, Baron of Darmouth in Devonshire, who is to be beheaded at the London Market-Place, for the crimes of regicide and high treason. God have mercy on his soul!

THE TWO STANDARD-BEARERS.

Pray for him!

[*The procession slowly crosses the back of the stage.*

JANE.

This is a terrible thing we are looking at, Joshua. It freezes my blood.

JOSHUA.

That abominable Fabiani!

JANE.

Peace, Joshua! Very abominable, but very unfortunate.

[*The procession reaches the other staircase: Simon Renard, who appeared at the entrance of this staircase, some moments before, and has observed everything, moves aside to let them pass. The procession goes under the arch of the staircase, and gradually disappears. Jane, terrified, follows it with her eyes.*

SIMON RENARD (*after the procession has disappeared*).

What does this mean? Is that really Fabiani? I thought him not so tall. Has Master Eneas?—It seems to me the Queen kept him near her for a moment. Let us see!

[*He disappears under the staircase, following the procession.*

VOICE (*which grows fainter and fainter*).

The man, covered with a black veil, who follows me, is the very high and mighty Lord Fabiano Fabiani, Earl of Clanbrassil, Baron of Dinasmonddy, Baron of Darmouth in Devonshire, who is to be beheaded at the London Market-Place, for the crimes of regicide and high treason.

OTHER VOICES (*almost indistinct*).

Pray for him!

JOSHUA.

The great bell will announce his exit from the Tower, presently. Perhaps you can make your escape now: I must try to find a way. Wait for me here: I will come back.

JANE.

Are you going to leave me, Joshua? I will be afraid here, all alone.

JOSHUA.

It will be dangerous for you to wander over the Tower with me. I must get you away from here. Remember Gilbert is waiting for you.

JANE.

Gilbert? Everything for Gilbert. Go!

[Joshua *goes out.*

Oh, what a terrible sight!—when I think that it might have been like this for Gilbert.

[*She kneels on one of the altar steps.*

Oh, thank you! You are indeed God the Saviour. You have saved Gilbert.

[*The cloth at the back opens.* The Queen *appears: she comes slowly to the front of the stage, without seeing* Jane, *who turns around.*

The Queen! My God!

SCENE II

JANE, THE QUEEN. JANE *clings to the altar, with horror, and fixes a look of stupor and terror on* THE QUEEN'S *face*

THE QUEEN (*she stands a few seconds at the front of the stage, her glance fixed, pale, as if absorbed in gloomy thoughts. At last she sighs profoundly*).

Oh, the people!

[*She looks around with anxiety and sees* Jane.

Some one is here. Oh, it is you, young woman! It is you, Lady Jane. I frighten you. Don't be afraid. You know the turnkey Eneas betrayed us. Don't be afraid. I have already told you, child, you have nothing to fear from me. What was your ruin a month ago is your salvation to-day. You love Fabiano. There are only you and I in the whole world to-day who have a heart like that. Only you and I love him. We are sisters.

JANE.

Madame—

THE QUEEN.

Yes, you and I—two women, we are all he has! Every one else is against him; a whole city, a whole nation, a whole world. Unequal struggle of love against hate. Love for Fabiano is a sad thing, a fatal, a horror-stricken thing: it has a pallid brow like yours, tear-filled eyes like mine; it hides itself close to a funereal altar; it entreats with your lips, it curses with mine. But hate for Fabiano is a proud thing, radiant, triumphant: it is well-armed and victorious; it has the Court, the people, the crowded streets; it munches cries of death and cries of joy at the same time; it is magnificent, haughty, powerful; it illuminates a whole city surrounding a scaffold. Love, here it is—two women weeping in a tomb! Hate, there it is!

[*She pulls the white cloth violently aside, which reveals a balcony, and beyond the balcony, almost out of sight, the whole city of London, brilliantly illuminated. What is visible of the Tower of London is also illuminated.* Jane *fixes her amazed eyes on this startling scene, the reflection of which lights up the theater.*

THE QUEEN.

Oh, infamous city; rebellious city; accursed city; monstrous city—who soaks her holiday dress in blood, and who holds the torch for the executioner! You are afraid of it, aren't you, Jane? Doesn't it seem to you, as it does to me, that it cowardly defies us both; that it is watching us with its hundred thousand flaming eyes—us, feeble, forsaken women that we are, alone and lost in this sepulcher? Jane, do you hear it howl and laugh—that horrible city? Oh, England, all England to him who will destroy London! Would that I could change those torches into fiery brands, those lights into flames, and that illuminated city into a city of *fire!*

[*A tremendous outburst from the people outside—applause, confused cries,* "There he is! There he is! Death to Fabiani—" *The great bell of the Tower begins to toll. At this sound,* The Queen *breaks into a terrible peal of laughter.*

JANE.

God! The unfortunate man is leaving the Tower!—You laugh, madame!

THE QUEEN.

Yes, I laugh! [*She laughs.*] Yes, and you will laugh, too. Let me drop those hangings first. It seems to me all the time as if we were not alone, as if that frightful city could see and hear us.

[*She drops the white curtain and comes back to* Jane.

Now that he is gone, now that there is no more danger, I can tell you about it. Laugh, laugh, let us both laugh at those execrable people who drink blood! Oh, it is grand, Jane! Jane, you tremble for Fabiano? Be at ease, laugh with me, I tell you. Jane, the man they've got, the man who is going to die, the man they think is Fabiano—is not Fabiano.

[*She laughs.*]

JANE.

Not Fabiano?

THE QUEEN.

No!

JANE.

Then who is it?

THE QUEEN.

The other!

JANE.

What other?

THE QUEEN.

You know well enough! You know him—that workman—that man. Besides, what does it matter?

JANE (*trembling with terror*).

Gilbert?

THE QUEEN.

Yes, Gilbert! That is the name.

JANE.

Madame! Oh, no, madame! Don't say that, madame! Gilbert—it would be too horrible! He has escaped!

THE QUEEN.

He was escaping when they seized him. They put him under the black veil in Fabiano's place. It is night. The people won't know. Rest easy.

JANE (*with a frightful cry*).

Ah, madame! But the man I love—it is Gilbert!

THE QUEEN.

What? What do you say? Are you going crazy? Did you deceive me, too? Ah, it is Gilbert whom you love! Well, what does that matter to me?

JANE (*at* The Queen's *feet, broken-hearted, sobbing, dragging herself on her knees, her hands clasped: the great bell tolls through all this scene*).

Madame—just for pity! Madame, in the name of Heaven!

Madame, by your crown, by your mother, by the angels! Gilbert, Gilbert—it will make me mad! Madame, save Gilbert! That man, he is my life; that man, he is my husband; that man— I have told you that he did everything for me, that he brought me up, that he adopted me, that beside my cradle he took the place of my father, who died for your father. Madame, you see that I am a poor, wretched creature, and it isn't right to be too hard on me. What you said to me just now struck such a terrible blow that I don't truly see how it is I have strength to speak to you. I am just saying what I can, you see. But you must stop the execution—right away! Stop the execution! Put it off until to-morrow. Just time to have things understood, that is all. The people can wait until to-morrow, I know. We will see what we can do. No! don't shake your head! There is no danger for your Fabiano. You can put me in his place—under the black veil—at night. Who will know? But you must save Gilbert. What difference does it make whether it be he or I? And since—since I want to die! Oh, my God, that bell, that frightful bell! Every knell of that bell is a step toward the scaffold. Every knell of that bell strikes me full in the heart. Do it, madame. Be merciful! No danger for your Fabiano! Let me kiss your hands. I love you, madame. I never said it before—but I love you dearly. You are a great queen. See, how I kiss your beautiful hands! Give an order to stop the execution. There is time yet. I am sure we can do it. They go so slowly. It is a long way from the Tower to the old Market-Place. The man on the balcony said they would pass through Charing Cross. There is a quicker way. A man on horseback could get there. In Heaven's name, madame, be merciful! Try to put yourself in my place.

Imagine that I am Queen and you the poor young woman; and you would weep as I do, and I would pardon. Pardon! Pardon! Oh, that is what I was afraid of, that my tears would hinder me from speaking! Oh, right away!—stop the execution! There won't be any trouble, madame; no danger for Fabiano, I swear it to you. Don't you really think you ought to do what I say, madame?

THE QUEEN (*touched and lifting her up*).

I wish I could, poor girl. Ah, yes, you are weeping as I wept; what you feel I have just felt myself, and my anguish makes me understand yours. Look! I am weeping too. It is very sad, my poor child. It seems to me, too, they might have taken somebody else—Tyrconnel, for instance. But he is too well known: they had to have some obscure man. He was the only one they could get hold of. I explain all this so that you can understand, don't you see? My God, there are fatalities like that: we get caught. We can't do anything.

JANE.

I am listening to you, madame. I am like you. I have got many things to say. But I would like to have the order to suspend the execution signed, and the man sent off. You see it would be finished then. We could talk better afterward. Oh, that bell! forever, that bell!

THE QUEEN.

What you want is impossible, Lady Jane.

JANE.

Oh, no, it is possible!—a man on horseback. There is a very short way—by the wharf. I can go—I— It is quite possible! It is easy! You see I talk very quietly.

THE QUEEN.

But the people won't have it. They will come back here and massacre everybody in the Tower. And Fabiano is here yet. Can't you understand? You are trembling, poor child. I am like you—I tremble also. In your turn, put yourself in my place. I might easily not take the trouble to explain all this to you. You see I do what I can. Don't think about this Gilbert any more. Jane, it is over— Resign yourself.

JANE.

Over! No, it is not over! No—as long as that horrible bell tolls, it is not over! Resign myself to Gilbert's death? Do you think I am going to let Gilbert die like that? No, madame! Ah, I am wasting my time! Ah, you won't listen to me! Very well, if the Queen won't hear me, the people will. They are good, the people—if you but knew it! They are in the court yet. You can do what you like with me afterward. I am going to tell them they are cheated; and that it is not Fabiani, it's a poor workman, named Gilbert—a workman like themselves!

THE QUEEN.

Stop, you wretched child!

[*She seizes her arm and looks at her fixedly and resentfully.*

This is the way you thank me, is it? I am patient and gentle with you, I weep with you—and all at once, you get wild and furious! Well, my love is just as great as yours, and my hand is more powerful! You shall not stir! Your lover!—what do I care for your lover? Are all the girls in England coming to ask me about their lovers, now? By my soul, I save my own as well as I can, and at the cost of everything which stands in his way. You must look after yours.

JANE.

Let me go! Oh, I curse you, you wretched, wicked woman!

THE QUEEN.

Hush!

JANE.

I will not hush! Do you want me to tell you what I'm thinking of now? I don't believe the man who is going to die out there is my Gilbert.

THE QUEEN.

What are you saying?

JANE.

I don't know, but I saw him pass by under that black veil; and if it had been my Gilbert, something would have stirred in me, something would have roused itself in my heart, and would have cried out to me, "Gilbert—it is Gilbert." But I felt nothing at all; it is not Gilbert.

THE QUEEN.

What are you saying? Ah, my God! you are crazy. What you have said is idiotic, but it terrifies me just the same. Ah, you have roused one of the secret terrors of my own heart! Why did that riot prevent me from looking after him myself? Why did I intrust to any one but myself the safety of my Fabiano? Eneas Dulverton is a traitor. Perhaps Simon Renard was there. What if I have been betrayed a second time by Fabiano's enemies? What if it is Fabiano himself? What, ho! quick—some one—come—some one!

[*Two Jailers appear.*

[*To the first.*] You—run! Here is my royal signet. Tell them to suspend the execution. To the old Market-Place; to the old Market-Place! There is a shorter way, you said, Jane.

JANE.

By the wharf.

THE QUEEN (*to Jailer*).

By the wharf. A horse—go quick!

[*The Jailer goes out.*

[*To the second Jailer.*] You—go at once to Edward the Confessor's Tower. The two cells of the condemned criminals are there. There is a man in one of them. Bring him here at once.

[*The Jailer goes out.*

I tremble; my knees sink under me; I have not strength enough to go myself. Ah, you have made me as mad as yourself! Miserable girl, you have made me as wretched as yourself. I curse you as you cursed me. My God, will the man get there in time? What a torturing anxiety! I can't see anything more. All is trouble in my soul. Does the bell toll yet? Is it for Gilbert? Is it for Fabiano?

JANE.

The bell ceases.

THE QUEEN.

Then the procession is on the place for the execution. Will the man get there in time?

[*A cannon-shot is heard.*

JANE.

Heaven!

THE QUEEN.

He is ascending the scaffold! [*Second cannon.* He is kneeling!

JANE.

It is horrible! [*Third cannon.*

BOTH.

Ah!

THE QUEEN.

There is only one alive now. In a moment we will know which one. My God, let the man who comes in be Fabiano!

JANE.

My God, let it be Gilbert!

[*The curtain at the back opens.* Simon Renard *appears, holding* Gilbert *by the hand.*

Gilbert! [*They rush into each other's arms.*

THE QUEEN.

And Fabiano?

SIMON RENARD.

Dead.

THE QUEEN.

Dead! Dead! Who has dared—

SIMON RENARD.

I have dared. I have saved the Queen of England.

MARION DE LORME

DRAMATIS PERSONÆ

MARION DE LORME.
DIDIER.
LOUIS XIII.
MARQUIS DE SAVERNY.
MARQUIS DE NANGIS.
L'ANGELY.
M. DE LAFFEMAS.
DUKE DE BELLEGARDE.
MARQUIS DE BRICHANTEAU, }
COUNT DE GASSÉ, }
VISCOUNT DE BOUCHAVANNES, } OFFICERS OF THE REGIMENT
CHEVALIER DE ROCHEBARON, } OF ANJOU.
COUNT DE VILLAC, }
CHEVALIER DE MONTPESAT, }
DUKE DE BEAUPRÉAU.
VISCOUNT DE ROHAN.
ABBÉ DE GONDI.
COUNT DE CHARNACÉ.
SCARAMOUCHE, }
GRACIEUX, } PROVINCIAL COMEDIANS.
TAILLEBRAS, }
COUNCILOR OF THE GREAT CHAMBER.
TOWN CRIER.   CAPTAIN.
A JAILER.   A REGISTRAR.
THE EXECUTIONER.   FIRST WORKMAN.
SECOND WORKMAN.   THIRD WORKMAN.
A LACKEY.   DAME ROSE.

Provincial Comedians, Guards, Populace, Nobles, Pages. 1638.

MARION DE LORME

ACT I.

THE MEETING

SCENE.—*Blois. A bed-chamber. A window opening on a balcony at the back. To the right, a table with a lamp, and an armchair. To the left a door, covered by a portière of tapestry. In the background a bed*

SCENE I

MARION DE LORME, *in a very elegant wrapper, sitting beside the table, embroidering.* MARQUIS DE SAVERNY, *very young man, blonde, without mustache, dressed in the latest fashion of 1638*

SAVERNY (*approaching* Marion *and trying to embrace her*).
    Let us be reconciled, my sweet Marie!

MARION (*pushing him away*).

Not such close reconciliation, please!

SAVERNY (*insisting*).

Just one kiss!

MARION (*angrily*).

Marquis!

SAVERNY.

What a rage! Your mouthHad sweeter manners, not so long ago!

MARION.

Ah, you forget!

SAVERNY.

No, I remember, dear.

MARION (*aside*).

The bore! the tiresome creature!

SAVERNY.

Speak, fair one!What does this swift, unkind departure mean?While all are seeking you at Place Royale,Why do you hide yourself at Blois? Traitress,What have you done here all these two long months?

MARION.

I do what pleases me, and what I wishIs right. I'm free, my lord!

SAVERNY.

Free! Yes. But thoseWhose hearts you've stolen, are they also free?I? Gondi, who omitted half his MassThe other day, because he had a duelUpon his hands for you? Nesmond, D'Arquien,The two Caussades, Pressigny, whom your flightHas left so wretched, so morose, evenTheir wives wish you were back in Paris, thatThey might have gayer husbands!

MARION (*smiling*).
　Beauvillain?
SAVERNY.
　Is still in love.
MARION.
　Cereste?
SAVERNY.
　Adores you yet.
MARION.
　And Pons?
SAVERNY.
　Oh, as for him, he hates you!
MARION.
　Proof
　He is the only one who loves me! Well,
　The President?[*Laughing.*] The old man! What's his name?
　　　[*Laughing more heartily.*
　Leloup!
SAVERNY.
　He's waiting for you, and meanwhileHe keeps your portrait and sings odes to it.
MARION.
　He's loved me two years now, in effigy.
SAVERNY.
　He'd much prefer to burn you. Tell me howYou keep away from such dear friends.
MARION (*serious, and lowering her eyes*).
　That's just
　The reason, Marquis; to be frank with you,
　Those brilliant follies which seduced my youth

Have given me much more misery than joy.
In a retreat, a convent cell, perhaps,
I want to try to expiate my life.
SAVERNY.
I'll wager there's a love-tale behind that.
MARION.
You dare to think—
SAVERNY.
That never a nun's veil
Surmounted eyes so full of earthly fire.
It could not be. You love some poor provincial!
For shame! To end a fine romance with such
A page!
MARION.
It isn't true!
SAVERNY.
Let's make a wager!
MARION.
Dame Rose, what time is it?
DAME ROSE (*outside*).
Almost midnight!
MARION (*aside*).
Midnight!
SAVERNY.
That is a most ingenious wayOf saying, "Time to go."
MARION.
I live retired,
Receiving no one, and unknown to all.
Besides, 'tis dangerous to be out late:
The street is lonely, full of robbers.

SAVERNY.

　Well, They can rob me.

MARION.

　And oftentimes they kill!

SAVERNY.

　Good! they can kill me.

MARION.

　But—

SAVERNY.

　You are divine!

　But I'll not stir one foot before I know

　Who this gay shepherd is, who's routed us!

MARION.

　There's no one!

SAVERNY.

　I will be discreet. We courtiers,

　Whom people think so mad, so curious

　And spiteful, are maligned. We gossip, but

　We never talk! You're silent?

　　　[*Sits down.*] Then I'll stay!

MARION.

　What does it matter? Well, it's true! I love!

　I'm waiting for him!

SAVERNY.

　That's the way to talk! That's right!

　Where is it you expect him?

MARION.

　Here!

SAVERNY.

　When?

MARION.

Now! [*She goes to the balcony and listens.*
   Hark! that is he perhaps.
         [*Coming back.*] 'Tis not.
Now are you satisfied?

SAVERNY.

Not quite!

MARION.

Please go!

SAVERNY.

I want to know his name, this proud gallant,
For whose reception I am thus dismissed.

MARION.

Didier is all the name I know for him.
Marie is all the name he knows for me.

SAVERNY (*laughing*).

Is't true?

MARION.

Yes, true!

SAVERNY.

               This is a pastoral,
And no mistake. 'Tis Racan, pure! To enter,
I have no doubt he scales the wall.

MARION.

Perhaps. Please go! [*Aside.*]
He wearies me to death!

SAVERNY (*becoming serious*).

   Of course
He's noble.

MARION.
 I don't know.
SAVERNY.
 What?
 [*To* Marion, *who is gently pushing him toward the door.*
  I am going! [*Coming back.*
 Just one word more! I had forgotten. Look!
 [*He draws a book out of his pocket and gives it to* MARION.
 An author who is not a fool, did this.
 It's making a great stir.
MARION (*reading the title*).
  "Love's Garland"—ah!
 "To Marion de Lorme."
SAVERNY.
  They talk of nothing
 But this in Paris. That book and "The Cid"
 Are the successful efforts of the day.
MARION (*taking the book*).
 It's very civil of you; now, good-night!
SAVERNY.
 What is the use of fame? Alack-a-day!
 To come to Blois and love a rustic! Bah!
MARION (*calling to* Dame Rose).
 Take care of the Marquis, and show him out!
SAVERNY (*saluting her*).
 Ah, Marion, you've degenerated! [*He goes out.*

SCENE II

Marion, *afterward* Didier

MARION (*alone, shuts the door by which* Saverny *went out*).
Go—
Go quickly! Oh, I feared lest Didier—
[*Midnight strikes.*
Hark!
It's striking midnight! Didier should be here!
[*She goes to the balcony and looks into the street.*
No one!
[*She comes back and sits down impatiently.*
Late! To be late—so soon!
[*A young man appears behind the balustrade of the balcony, jumps over it lightly, enters, places his cloak and sword on the armchair. Costume of the day: all black: boots. He takes one step forward, pauses and contemplates* Marion, *sitting with her eyes cast down.*
At last!
[*Reproachfully.*
To let me count the hour alone!
DIDIER (*seriously*).
I fearedTo enter!
MARION (*hurt*).
Ah!
DIDIER (*without noticing it*).
Down there, outside the wall,
I was o'ercome with pity. Pity? yes,
For you! I, poor, accursed, unfortunate,
Stood there a long time thinking, ere I came!"

Up there an angel waits," I thought, "in virgin grace,
Untouched by sin—a being chaste and fair,
To whose sweet face shining on life's pathway
Each passer-by should bend his knees and pray.
I, who am but a vagrant 'mongst the crowd,
Why should I seek to stir that placid stream?
Why should I pluck that lily? With the breath
Of human passion, why should I consent
To cloud the azure of that radiant soul?
Since in her loyalty she trusts to me,
Since virtue shields her with its sanctity,
Have I a right to take her gift of love,
To bring my storms into her perfect day?"

MARION (*aside*).
   This is theology, it seems to me!
   I wonder if he is a Huguenot?

DIDIER.
   But when your tender voice fell on my ear,
   I wrestled with my doubts no more—I came.

MARION.
   Oh, then you heard me speaking—that is strange!

DIDIER.
   Yes; with another person.

MARION (*quickly*).
   With Dame Rose!
   She talks just like a man, don't you think so?
   Such a strong voice! Ah, well, since you are here
   I am no longer angry! Come, sit down.
   [*Indicating a place at her side.*
   Sit here!

DIDIER.

No! at your feet.

[*He sits on a stool at* MARION's *feet and looks at her for some moments in complete silence.*

          Hear me, Marie!
I have no name but Didier—never knew
My father nor my mother. I was left,
A baby, on the threshold of a church.
A woman, old, belonging to the people,
Preserved me, was my mother and my nurse.
She brought me up a Christian, then she died
And left me all she had—nine hundred francs
A year, on which I live. To be alone
At twenty is a sad and bitter thing!
I traveled—saw mankind: I learned to hate
A few and to despise the rest. For on
This tarnished mirror we call human life,
I saw nothing but pride and misery
And pain; so that, although I'm young, I'm old,
And am as weary of the world as are
The men who leave it. Never touched a thing
That did not tear and lacerate my soul!
Although the world was bad, I found men worse.
Thus I have lived; alone and poor and sad,
Until you came, and you have set things right.
I hardly know you. At the corner of
A Paris street you first appeared to me.
Then afterward I met you, and I thought
Your eyes were sweet, your speech was beautiful!
I was afraid of loving you, and fled!

But destiny is strange: I found you here,
I find you everywhere, as if you were
My guardian angel. So at last, my love
Grew powerful, resistless, and I felt
I must talk with you. You were willing. Now
They're at your service, both my heart and life.
I will do anything that you wish done.
If there is any man or anything
That troubles you, or you have any whim
And somebody must die to satisfy it—
Must die, and make no sign—and feel 'twas worth
Death any time to see you smile; if you
Need such a man, speak, lady: I am here!

MARION (*smiling*).

You've a strange nature, but I love you so!

DIDIER.

You love me! Ah, take care! One dare not say
Such words in any careless way! Love me?
Oh, do you know what loving means? What 'tis
To feel love take possession of our blood,
Become our daily breath? To feel this thing
Which long has smoldered burst to flame, and rise
A great, majestic, purifying fire?
To feel it burn up clean within our hearts
The refuse other passions have left there?
This love, hopeless indeed, but limitless,
Which outlives all things, even happiness—
Is this the kind of love you mean?

MARION (*touched*).

Indeed!

DIDIER.
> You do not know it, but I love you so!
> From that first time I saw you, my dark life
> Was shot with sunlight streaming from your eyes;
> Since then all's different. To me you seem
> Some wonderful creation, not of earth.
> My life, in whose dark gloom I groaned so long,
> Grows almost beautiful when you are by.
> For 'til you came, I'd wandered, suffered, wept;
> I'd struggled, fallen—but I had not loved.

MARION.
> Poor Didier!

DIDIER.
> > Speak, Marie!

MARION.
> Well, then, I do.
> I love with just this love—love you as much
> And maybe more than you love me! It was
> Not destiny that brought me here. 'Twas I
> Who came, who followed you, and I am yours!

DIDIER (*falling on his knees*).
> Oh, do not cheat me! Give me truth, Marie!
> If to my ardent love your love responds,
> The world holds no possession rich as mine!
> My whole life, kneeling at your feet, will be
> One sigh of speechless, blinding ecstasy.
> But do not cheat me!

MARION.
> > Do you want a proof
> Of love, my Didier?

DIDIER.
   Yes!
MARION.
   Then speak!
DIDIER.
   You are—Quite free?
MARION (*embarrassed*).
   Free? Yes!
DIDIER.
   Then take me for a brother,For a protector—be my wife?
MARION (*aside*).
   His wife!Ah, why am I not worthy?
DIDIER.
   You consent?
MARION.
   I—can—
DIDIER.
   Don't say it, please—I understand!
   An orphan, without fortune! What a fool!
   Give back my pain, my gloom, my solitude!
   Farewell!
   [*He starts to go;* Marion *holds him back.*
MARION.
   Didier, what are you saying?
   [*She bursts into tears.*
DIDIER.
   True!
   But why this hesitation? [*Going back to her.*
               Can't you feel
   The ecstasy of being, each to each, a world,

    A country, heaven; in some deserted spot
    To hide a happiness kings could not buy.
MARION.
    It would be heaven!
DIDIER.
    Will you have it? Come!
MARION.
    [*Aside.*] Accursed woman! [*Aloud.*] No, it cannot be.
    [*She tears herself from out his arms, and falls on the armchair.*
DIDIER (*freezingly*).
    The offer was not generous, I know.
    You've answered me. I'll speak of it no more!
    Good-by!
MARION. (*aside*).
    Alack, the day I pleased him! [*Aloud.*] Stay!
    I'll tell you. You have hurt me to the soul.
    I will explain—
DIDIER (*coldly*).
    What were you reading, madame,
    When I came?
    [*Takes the book from the table and reads.*
    "To Marion de Lorme.
    Love's Garland!" Yes, the beauty of the day!
    [*Throwing the book violently to the floor.*
    Vile creature! a dishonor to her sex!
MARION. (*trembling*).
    But—she—
DIDIER.
    What are you doing with such books?
    How came they here?

MARION. (*inaudibly, and looking down*).
  They came by chance.
DIDIER.
  Do you—
  You who have eyes so pure, a brow so chaste—
  Do you know what she is—this woman? Well,
  She's beautiful in body, and deformed
  In soul! A Phryne, selling everywhere,
  To every man, her love, which is an insult,
  An infamy!
MARION (*her head in her hands*).
  My God!
  [*A noise of footsteps, a clashing of swords outside, and cries.*
VOICE IN THE STREET.
  Help! Murder! Help!
DIDIER (*surprised*).
  What noise is that out there upon the square?
  [*Cries continue.*
VOICE IN THE STREET.
  Help! Murder! Help!
DIDIER (*looking from the balcony*).
  They're killing some one! Ha!
  [*He takes his sword and step's over the balustrade.* MARION *rises, runs to him and tries to hold him back by his cloak.*
MARION.
  Don't, Didier, if you love me! They'll kill you! Don't go!
DIDIER (*jumping down into the street*).
  He is the one they're going to kill!
  Poor man! [Outside, to combatants.
  Stand off! Hold firmly, sir, and push!

[Clashing of swords.

There, wretch!

MARION. (*on the balcony, terrified*).

Just Heaven! They are six 'gainst two!

VOICE IN THE STREET.

This man—he is the devil!

[*The clashing of swords subsides little by little, then entirely ceases. The sounds of footsteps become indistinct.* DIDIER *reappears scaling the balcony.*

DIDIER (*outside of the balcony and turned toward the street*).

You are safe;Now go your way!

SAVERNY (*from outside*).

Not 'til I've grasped your hand—

Not 'til I've thanked you, if you please!

DIDIER.

Pass on!I will consider myself thanked.

SAVERNY.

Not so!I mean to thank you. [*Scaling balcony.*

DIDIER.

Can't you speak from there

And say "I thank you" without coming up?

SCENE III

MARION, DIDIER, SAVERNY

SAVERNY (*jumping into the room, sword in hand*).

Upon my soul! 'Tis a strange chivalry

To save my life and push me from the door!
The door—that is to say, the window! No,
They shall not say one of my family
Was bravely rescued by a nobleman
And did not in return say "Marquis—" Pray,
What is your name?

DIDIER.
　Didier.

SAVERNY.
　Didier—of what?

DIDIER.
　Didier, of nothing! People kill you, and
I help you—that is all! Now go!

SAVERNY.
　Indeed!
That's your way, is it? Why not have let
Those traitors kill me? 'Twould have pleased me more.
For without you I'd be a dead man now.
Six thieves against me! Dead! Of course! What else?
Six daggers against one thin sword—
[Perceiving Marion, who has been trying to avoid him.
Oh, ho!
You're not alone! At last I understand!
I'm robbing you of pleasure. Pardon me!
[Aside.] I'd like to see the lady!
[Approaches Marion, who is trembling: he recognizes her.
It is you!
[Indicating Didier.
Then he's the one!

MARION (*low*).

Hush! You will ruin all!

SAVERNY (*bowing*).

Madame!

MARION (*low*).

I love for the first time!

DIDIER (*aside*).

'Sdeath!

That man is looking at her with bold eyes.

[*He overturns the lamp with a blow.*

SAVERNY.

You put the lamp out, sir?

DIDIER.

It would be wiseFor us to leave together, and at once.

SAVERNY.

So be it, then! I follow you!

[*To* Marion, *whom he salutes profoundly.*

Madame,Farewell!

DIDIER (*aside*).

What a rare coxcomb![*Aloud to* Saverny.] Come, sir, come!

SAVERNY.

You're brusk, but I'm in debt to you for life.

If ever you should need fraternal friendship,

Count upon me, Marquis de Saverny,

Paris, Hôtel de Nesle.

DIDIER.

Enough, sir! Come![*Aside.*] To see her thus examined by a fool!

[*They go out by the balcony. The voice of* DIDIER *is heard outside.*

Your road lies that way. Mine lies here!

SCENE IV

Marion, Dame Rose

MARION (*remains absorbed a moment, then calls*).
  Dame Rose!
  [DAME ROSE *appears.* MARION *points to the window.*
  Go shut it!
  [DAME ROSE, *having shut the window, turns and sees* MARION *wiping away a tear.*
DAME ROSE (*aside*).
  She is weeping![*Aloud.*] It is timeTo sleep, madame!
MARION.
  Yes, time for you—you people.
  [*Undoing her hair.*
  Come, help me to undress!
DAME ROSE (*helping her to undress*).
  The gentlemanTo-night was pleasant. Is he rich?
MARION.
  Not rich.
DAME ROSE.
  But gallant.
MARION.
  No, nor gallant.
  [*Turning to* Dame Rose.
  He did notSo much as kiss my hand!

DAME ROSE.
   What use is he?
MARION (*pensive*).
   I love him!

MARION DE LORME.

ACT II.

THE ENCOUNTER

SCENE.—*Blois. The door of a public-house. A square. In the background the city of Blois is visible in the form of an amphitheater, also the towers of St. Nicholas upon the hill, which is covered with houses*

SCENE I

COUNT DE GASSÉ, MARQUIS DE BRICHANTEAU, VISCOUNT DE BOUCHAVANNES, CHEVALIER DE ROCHEBARON. *They are seated at tables in front of the door: some are smoking, the others are throwing dice and drinking. Afterward* CHEVALIER DE MONTPESAT, COUNT DE VILLAC; *afterward* L'ANGELY; *afterward* THE TOWN-CRIER *and The Populace*

BRICHANTEAU (*rising, to* Gassé, *who enters*).
Gassé! [They shake hands.
You are come to join
The regiment at Blois: our compliments
Upon your burial. [Examining his clothes.
Ah!
GASSÉ.
It is the style—
This orange with blue ribbons.
[Folding his arms and curling his mustache.

You must know
That Blois is forty miles from Paris!
BRICHANTEAU.
Yes, It's China!
GASSÉ.
That makes womankind rebel:
To follow us they must exile themselves.
BOUCHAVANNES (*turning from the game*).
You come from Paris?
ROCHEBARON (*taking out his pipe*).
Is there any news?
GASSÉ (*bowing*).
No, nothing. Corneille still upsets all heads.
Guiche has obtained the order; Ast is duke.
Of trifles, plenty—thirty Huguenots
Were hung; a quantity of duels. On
The third, D'Angennes fought Arquien on account
Of wearing point of Genoa; the tenth,
Lavardie had a rendezvous with Pons,
Because he'd taken Sourdis' wife from him.
Sourdis and D'Ailly met about a creature
In the theater Mondori. On the ninth,
Lachâtre fought with Nogent because he wrote
Three rhymes of Colletet's badly; Margaillan
With Gorde, about the time of day; D'Humière
With Gondi on the way to walk in church;
And all the Brissacs 'gainst all the Soubises
For some bet on a horse against a dog.
Then Caussade and Latournelle fought for nothing—
Merely for fun: Caussade killed Latournelle.

BRICHANTEAU.

　Gay Paris! Duels have begun again.

GASSÉ.

　It is the fashion!

BRICHANTEAU.

　Feasts and love and fighting!

　There is the only place to live!

　[*Yawning.*] All one

　Can do here is to die of weariness.

　[*To* GASSÉ.] You say Caussade killed Latournelle?

GASSÉ.

　He did,

　With a good gash!

　[Examining ROCHEBARON'S *sleeves.*

　What's that you wear, my friend?

　Those trimmings are not fashionable now.

　What! cords and buttons? Nothing could be worse.

　You must have bows and ribbons.

BRICHANTEAU.

　Pray repeat

　The list of duels. How about the King?

　What does he say?

GASSÉ.

　The Cardinal's enraged

　And means to stop it.

BOUCHAVANNES.

　Any news from camp?

GASSÉ.

　I think we captured Figuère by surprise—

　Or else we lost it.

[*Reflecting.*] Yes, that's it. 'Tis lost!
They took it from us.
ROCHEBARON.
Ah! What said the King?
GASSÉ.
The Cardinal is most dissatisfied.
BRICHANTEAU.
How is the Court? I hope the King is well.
GASSÉ.
Alas! the Cardinal has fever and
The gout, and goes out only in a litter.
BRICHANTEAU.
Queer! We talk King, you answer Cardinal!
GASSÉ.
It is the fashion!
BOUCHAVANNES.
So there's nothing new!
GASSÉ.
Did I say so? There's been a miracle,
A prodigy, which has amazed all Paris
For two months past; the flight, the disappearance—
BRICHANTEAU.
Go on! Of whom?
GASSÉ.
Of Marion de Lorme,
The fairest of the fair!
BRICHANTEAU (*with an air of mystery*).
Here's news for you. She's here!
GASSÉ.
At Blois?

BRICHANTEAU.
  Incognito!
GASSÉ.
  What! she?
  In this place? Oh, you must be jesting, sir!
  Fair Marion, who sets the fashions! Bah!
  This Blois is the antipodes of Paris.
  Observe! How ugly, old, ungainly, 'tis!
  Even those towers—
  [Indicating the towers of St. Nicholas.
  Uncouth and countrified!
ROCHEBARON.
  That's true.
BRICHANTEAU.
  Won't you believe Saverny when
  He says he saw her, hidden somewhere with
  A lover, and this lover saved his life
  When thieves attacked him in the street at night?—
  Good thieves, who took his purse for charity,
  And just desired his watch to know the time.
GASSÉ.
  You tell me wonders!
ROCHEBARON (*to* BRICHANTEAU).
  Are you sure of it?
BRICHANTEAU.
  As sure as that I have six silver bezants
  Upon a field of azure. Saverny
  Has no desire, at present, but to find
  This man.

BOUCHAVANNES.

He ought to find him at her house.

BRICHANTEAU.

She's changed her name and lodging, and all trace
Of her is lost.

[MARION *and* DIDIER *cross the back of the stage slowly without being noticed by the talkers; they enter a small door in one of the houses on the side.*

GASSÉ.

To have to come to Blois
To find our Marion, a provincial!

[*Enter* COUNT DE VILLAC *and* CHEVALIER DE MONTPESAT, *disputing loudly.*

VILLAC.

No! I tell you no!

MONTPESAT.

And I—I tell you, yes!

VILLAC.

Corneille is bad!

MONTPESAT.

To treat Corneille like that—
The author of "The Cid" and of "Melite."

VILLAC.

"Melite"? Well, I will grant you that is good;
But he degenerated after that,
As they all do. I'll do the best I can
To satisfy you: talk about "Melite,"
"The Gallery of the Palace," but "The Cid!"
What is it, pray?

GASSÉ (*to* MONTPESAT).

You are conservative.

MONTPESAT.

"The Cid" is good!

VILLAC.

I tell you it is bad!
Your "Cid"—why Scudéry can crush it with
A touch! Look at the style! It deals with things
Extraordinary; has a vulgar tone;
Describes things plainly by their common names;
Besides, it is obscene, against the law!
"The Cid" has not the right to wed Chimène!
Now have you read Pyramus, Bradamante?
When Corneille writes such tragedies, I'll read!

ROCHEBARON (*to* Montpesat).

"The Great and Last Soliman" of Mairet,
You must read that: that is fine tragedy!
But for your "Cid."

VILLAC.

What self-conceit he has!
Does he not think he equals Boisrobert,
Mairet, Gombault, Serisay, Chapelain,
Bautru, Desmarets, Malleville, Faret,
Cherisy, Gomberville, Colletet, Giry,
Duryer—indeed, all the Academy?

BRICHANTEAU (*laughing compassionately and shrugging his shoulders*).

Good!

VILLAC.

Then the gentleman deigns to create!

Create! Faith! after Garnier, Theophile,
And Hardy! Oh, the coxcomb! To create!
An easy thing! As if the famous minds
Had left behind them any unused thing.
On that point Chapelain rebukes him well!

ROCHEBARON.
Corneille's a peasant!

BOUCHAVANNES.
Yet, Monsieur Godeau,
Bishop of Grasse, says he's a man of wit.

MONTPESAT.
Much wit!

VILLAC.
If he would write some other way—
Would follow Aristotle and good style.

GASSÉ.
Come, gentlemen, make peace. One thing is sure,
Corneille is now the fashion: takes the place
Of Garnier, just as in our day felt hats
Have replaced velvet *mortiers*.

MONTPESAT.
For Corneille
I am, and for felt hats!

GASSÉ (*to* Montpesat).
You are too rash!
[*To* VILLAC.] Garnier is very fine. I'm neutral; but
Corneille has also his good points.

VILLAC.
Agreed!

ROCHEBARON.
   Agreed! He is a witty fellow and I like him!
BRICHANTEAU.
   He has no nobility!
ROCHEBARON.
   A name so commonplace offends the ear.
BOUCHAVANNES.
   A family of petty lawyers, who
   Have gnawed at ducats 'til they obtained sous.
   [*L'Angely enters, seats himself at a table alone, and in silence.*
   He is dressed in black velvet with gold trimming.
VILLAC.
   Well, if the public like his rhapsodies
   The day of tragic-comedy is past.
   I swear to you the theater is doomed.
   It is because this Richelieu—
GASSÉ (*looking across at L'Angely*).
   Say, *lordship*,
   Or else speak lower.
BRICHANTEAU.
   Hell take this eminence!
   Is't not enough to manage everything?
   To rule our soldiers, finances, and us,
   Without controlling our poor language too?
BOUCHAVANNES.
   Down with this Richelieu, who flatters, kills:
   Man of the red hand and the scarlet robe!
ROCHEBARON.
   Of what use is the King?

BRICHANTEAU.
   In darkness, we—
   That is the people—march: eyes on a torch.
   He is the torch: the King's the lantern which
   In its bright glass protects the flame from wind.
BOUCHAVANNES.
   Oh, could our swords blow such a wind some day
   As to extinguish this devouring fire!
ROCHEBARON.
   If every one had the same mind as I!
BRICHANTEAU.
   We would unite—
   [*To* BOUCHAVANNES.] What do you think, Viscount?
BOUCHAVANNES.
   We'd give him one perfidious, useful blow!
L'ANGELY (*rising, with gloomy tone*).
   Conspiring! Young men! Think of Marillac!
   [*All shudder: turn away, and are silent with terror; all fix their eyes on* L'Angely, *who silently resumes his seat.*
VILLAC (*taking* Montpesat *aside*).
   My lord, when we were talking of Corneille,
   You spoke in tones that irritated me.
   In my turn I would like to say two words
   To you—
MONTPESAT.
   With sword—
VILLAC.
   Yes.
MONTPESAT.
   Or with pistol?

VILLAC.

Both!

MONTPESAT (*taking his arm*).

Let's go and find some corner in the town.

L'ANGELY (*rising*).

A duel, sirs? Remember Boutteville.

[*New consternation among the young men.* VILLAC *and* Montpesat *separate, keeping their eyes fixed on* L'ANGELY.

ROCHEBARON.

Who is this man in black who frightens us?

L'ANGELY.

I'm L'Angely. I'm jester to the King.

BRICHANTEAU (*laughing*).

Then it's no wonder that the King is sad.

BOUCHAVANNES (*laughing*).

Great fun he makes, this rabid cardinalist!

L'ANGELY (*standing*).

Be careful, gentlemen! This minister
Is mighty. A great mower, he! He makes
Great seas of blood, and then he covers them
With his red cloak and nothing more is said. [*Silence.*

GASSÉ.

Good faith!

ROCHEBARON.

I'm blessed if I shall stir!

BRICHANTEAU.

Beside
This jester Pluto was a funny man!

[*A crowd of people enter from the streets and houses, and spread over the Square. In the center appears* THE TOWN-

CRIER *on horseback, with four Town-servants in livery, one of whom blows the trumpet, while the other beats the drum.*
GASSÉ.

What are these people doing? Ah, the crier!

Well, paternosters are in order now!

BRICHANTEAU (*to a juggler with a monkey on his back, who has joined the crowd*).

Which one of you shows off the other, friend?

MONTPESAT (*to* Rochebaron).

I hope our packs of cards are still complete.

[*Indicating the four Servants in livery.*

It looks as though these knaves were stolen thence.

TOWN-CRIER (*in a nasal tone of voice*).

Peace, citizens!

BRICHANTEAU (*low to* Gassé).

He has a wicked look.

His voice wears out his nose more than his mouth!

TOWN-CRIER.

"Ordinance: Louis, by the Grace of God—"

BOUCHAVANNES (*low to* Brichanteau).

Cloak *fleur-de-lis* concealing Richelieu!

L'ANGELY.

Attention!

TOWN-CRIER (*continuing*).

"King of France and of Navarre—"

BRICHANTEAU (*low to* Bouchavannes).

A fine name, which no minister e'er hoards.

TOWN-CRIER (*continuing*).

"Know all men by these presents, we greet you!

[*He salutes assembly.*

Having considered that all kings desired
And have tried to abolish dueling,
But yet, in spite of edicts signed by them,
The evil has increased in great degree,
We ordain and decree that from this time
All duelists who rob us of our subjects,
Whether but one of them or both survive,
Be brought for punishment unto our court,
And commoner or noble shall be hanged.
In order to give force to this edict
We here renounce our right of pardon for
This crime. It is our gracious pleasure."—
Signed, Louis; and lower—Richelieu.

[*Indignation among the nobles.*
BRICHANTEAU.
    What's this?
We are to hang up like Barabbas!
BOUCHAVANNES.
    We?
Tell me the name of any place which holds
A rope by which to hang a nobleman!
TOWN-CRIER (*continuing*).
"We, provost, that all men may know these facts,
Command this edict to be hung up on
The Square."
[*The two Servants attach a great placard to an iron gallows protruding from the wall on the right.*
GASSÉ.
    'Tis the edict they ought to hang!
Well done!

BOUCHAVANNES (*shaking his head*).
>Yes, Count; while waiting for the head
Which shall defy it.
[THE TOWN-CRIER *exits; the crowd retires.* SAVERNY *enters. It begins to grow dark.*

SCENE II

The same. MARQUIS DE SAVERNY

BRICHANTEAU (*going to* Saverny).
>Cousin Saverny,
I hope you've found the man who rescued you.
SAVERNY.
No; I have searched the city through in vain.
The robbers, the young man, and Marion—
They have all faded from me like a dream.
BRICHANTEAU.
You must have seen him when he brought you back,
Like a good Christian, from those infidels.
SAVERNY.
The first thing that he did was to throw down
The lamp.
GASSÉ.
That's strange!
BRICHANTEAU.
You'd recognize him if
You met him?

SAVERNY.

No; I didn't see his face.

BRICHANTEAU.

What is his name?

SAVERNY.

Didier.

ROCHEBARON.

That's no man's name!

That is a bourgeois name.

SAVERNY.

It doesn't matter.

Didier is this man's name. There are great men

Who have been conquerors and bear grand names,

But they've no greater hearts than this man had.

I had six robbers! He had Marion!

He left her, and saved me. My debt's immense!

This debt I mean to pay. I tell you all:

I'll pay it with the last drop of my blood!

VILLAC.

Since when do you pay debts?

SAVERNY (*proudly*).

I've always paid

Those debts which can be paid with blood.

Blood is the only change I carry, sir!

[*It is quite dark; the windows in the city are lighted one by one; a lamplighter enters and lights a street-lamp above the edict and goes out. The little door through which* MARION *and* DIDIER *disappeared is re-opened.* DIDIER *comes forth dreamily, walking slowly, his arms folded.*

SCENE III

The same. DIDIER

DIDIER (*coming slowly from the back; no one sees or hears him*).
   Marquis de Saverny! I would like much
   To see that fool who looked at her so hard.
   I have him on my mind.
BOUCHAVANNES (*to* SAVERNY, *who is talking with Brichanteau*).
   Saverny!
DIDIER (*aside*).
   Ah,
   That is my man!
[*He advances slowly, his eyes fixed on the noblemen, and sits down at a table placed under the street-lamp, which lights up the edict.* L'Angely, *motionless and silent, is a few steps distant.*
BOUCHAVANNES (*to* Saverny, *who turns around*).
   You know about the edict?
SAVERNY.
   Which one?
BOUCHAVANNES.
   Commanding us to give up duels.
SAVERNY.
   It is most wise.
BRICHANTEAU.
   Hanging's the penalty.

SAVERNY.

You must be jesting. Commoners are hanged, Not nobles.

BRICHANTEAU (*showing the placard*).

Read it for yourself. It's there, Upon the wall.

SAVERNY (*perceiving* Didier).

    That sallow face can read

For me.

    [To DIDIER, elevating his voice.

        Ho! man there with the cloak! My friend!

Good fellow!

[To BRICHANTEAU.] Brichanteau, he must be deaf.

DIDIER (*slowly lifting his head, without taking his eyes from him*).

You spoke to me?

SAVERNY.

I did! In fair return,

Read that placard which hangs above your head.

DIDIER.

I?

SAVERNY.

You—if you can spell the alphabet.

DIDIER (*rising*).

It is the edict threatening duelists

With gallows, be they nobles or plebeians.

SAVERNY.

No, you mistake, my friend. You ought to know

A nobleman was never born to hang,

And in this world, where we claim all our rights,

Plebeians are the gallows' only prey.

[*To the noblemen.*

These commoners are rude.
[*To* DIDIER, *with malice.*] You don't read well;
Perhaps you are near-sighted. Lift your hat,
'Twill give you more light. Take it off.

DIDIER (*overthrowing the table which is in front of him*).
    Beware!
You have insulted me! I've read for you;
I claim my recompense! I'll have it, too!
I want your blood, I want your head, Marquis!

SAVERNY (*smiling*).
We must be fitted to our station, sir.
I judge him commoner, he scents marquis
In me.

DIDIER.
Marquis and commoner can fight.
What do you say to mixing up our blood?

SAVERNY.
You go too fast, and fighting is not all.
I am Gaspard, Marquis de Saverny.

DIDIER.
What does that matter?

SAVERNY.
Here my seconds are!
The Count de Gassé, noble family,
And Count de Villac, family La Teuillade,
From which house comes the Marquis d'Aubusson.
Are you of noble blood?

DIDIER.
What matters that?
I am a foundling left at a church door.

I have no name; but in its place, I've blood,
To give you in exchange for yours!
SAVERNY.
That, sir,
Is not enough; but as a foundling, you
May claim the right, because you might be noble.
It is a better thing to lift a vassal
Than to degrade a peer. You may command me!
Choose your hour, sir.
DIDIER.
Immediately!
SAVERNY.
Agreed! You're no usurper, that is clear.
DIDIER.
A sword!
SAVERNY.
You have no sword? The devil! that is bad.
You might be thought a man of low descent.
Will you have mine?
[*Offers his sword to* DIDIER.
Well tempered and obedient!
[L'ANGELY *rises, draws his sword and presents it to* DIDIER.
L'ANGLEY.
No; for a foolish deed, you'd better take
A fool's sword! You are brave! You'll honor it!
[MALICIOUSLY.] And in return, to bring me luck, pray let
Me cut a piece from off the hanging-rope!
DIDIER (*bitterly, taking sword*).
I will.
[*To* THE MARQUIS.

Now God have mercy on the good!
BRICHANTEAU (*jumping with delight*).
A duel—excellent!
SAVERNY (*to* Didier).
Where shall we fight?
DIDIER.
Beneath the street-lamp.
GASSÉ.
Gentlemen, you're mad!
You cannot see. You'll put your eyes out.
DIDIER.
Humph!
There's light enough to cut each other's throat.
SAVERNY.
Well said!
VILLAC.
You can see nothing.
DIDIER.
That's enough!
Each sword is lightning flashing in the dark.
Come, Marquis!
[*Both throw off their cloaks, take off their hats with which they salute each other, throwing them afterward on the ground. Then they draw their swords.*
SAVERNY.
At your service, sir.
DIDIER.
Now! *Garde!*
[*They cross swords and fence, silently and furiously. Suddenly the small door opens, Marion in a white dress appears.*

SCENE IV

The same. MARION

MARION.
  What is this noise?
  [*Perceiving* Didier *under the lamp.*]
  Didier!
  [*To the combatants.*] Stop!
  [*They continue.*] Ho! The guard!
SAVERNY.
  Who is this woman?
DIDIER (*turning*).
  Heaven!
BOUCHAVANNES (*running, to* SAVERNY).
  All is lost!
  That woman's cry went through the town.
  I saw the archers' rapiers flash.
  [*The Archers with torches enter.*]
BRICHANTEAU (*to* SAVERNY).
  Seem dead,
  Or you will be so!
SAVERNY (*falling down*).
  Ah!
  [*Low to* BRICHANTEAU, *who bends over him.*]
  Oh, damn these stones.
  [Didier, *who thinks he has killed him, pauses.*]
CAPTAIN OF THE DISTRICT.
  Hold! In the King's name!

BRICHANTEAU (*to the noblemen*).
> We must save the Marquis.
> He's a dead man if he is caught.
> [*The noblemen surround* Saverny.

CAPTAIN OF THE DISTRICT.
> Zounds, sirs!
> To fight a duel 'neath the very light
> Of the edict is bold indeed!
> [*To* Didier.] Give up
> Your sword.
> [*The Archers seize* Didier, *who stands apart, and disarm him. The Captain* indicates Saverny *stretched upon the ground and surrounded by the noblemen.*
> That other man with dull eyes, who
> Is he? What is his name?

BRICHANTEAU.
> His name's Gaspard,
> Marquis de Saverny, and he is dead.

CAPTAIN OF THE DISTRICT.
> Dead, is he? Then his trouble's over. Good!
> This dead man's worth more than the other.

MARION (*frightened*).
> What!

CAPTAIN OF THE DISTRICT (*to* Didier).
> The whole affair rests now with you, sir. Come!
> [*The Archers lead* Didier *off on one side, the noblemen carry* Saverny *off on the other.*

DIDIER (*to* MARION, *who is motionless from horror*).
> Forget me, Marion. Good-by! [*They exit.*

SCENE V

MARION, L'ANGELY

MARION (*rushing to detain him*).
Didier!
What do you mean? Good-by? Why this good-by?
Wherefore forget you?
[*The Soldiers push her off; she approaches* L'ANGELY *with anguish.*
Is he lost for this?
What did he do? What will they do to him?
L'ANGELY (*takes her hand and leads her in silence before the edict*).
Read this!
MARION (*reads, and starts back with horror*).
My God! Just God! Condemned to death!
They've taken him away. To kill him! Oh,
I brought this ruin on him with my cries!
I called for help, but my unhappy voice
Found death in the dark streets and brought her here.
Impossible! A duel is no crime!
[*To* L'ANGELY.
They'll not kill him for that?
L'ANGELY.
I think they will.
MARION.
He can escape!

L'ANGELY.

The prison walls are high!

MARION.

I've brought this crime upon him with my sins.

God strikes him for my sake! My Didier! love!

[*To* L'ANGELY.] Nothing on earth seemed good enough for him!

A prison cell—my God! Death! Torture too!

L'ANGELY.

Perhaps! It all depends—

MARION.

I'll find the King! He has a royal heart; he pardons.

L'ANGELY.

Yes, The King does, not the Cardinal.

MARION.

Then, what—What can I do?

L'ANGELY.

A capital offense, Nothing can save him from the fatal rope.

MARION.

Oh, grief! [*To* L'ANGELY.] You freeze my blood, sir. Who are you?

L'ANGELY.

I'm the King's jester!

MARION.

Oh, my Didier, love,

I'm lost, unworthy; but what God can do

With a weak woman's hands, I'll show to you.

Go on, my love; I follow!

[*She goes out on the side from which* DIDIER *left.*

L'ANGELY (*alone*).
  God knows where!
  [*Picking up the sword which* DIDIER *left on the ground.*
  Among all these, who'd think I was the fool?
  [*He goes out.*

ACT III.

THE COMEDY

SCENE.—*The Castle of Nangis. A park in the style of Henry IV. In the background on an elevation, the Castle of Nangis, part new, part old, is visible. The old, a castle-keep with arches and turrets: the new, a large brick house with corners of wrought stone, and pointed roof. The large door of the castle-keep is hung with black: from afar one distinguishes a coat-of-arms—that of the families of Nangis and of Saverny*

SCENE I

M. DE LAFFEMAS, *undress costume of a magistrate of the period.* MARQUIS DE SAVERNY, *disguised as an officer of the Regiment of Anjou; with black mustache and imperial, and a plaster on the eye*

LAFFEMAS.

Then you were present, sir, at the attack?

SAVERNY (*pulling his mustache*).

I was his comrade: had that honor, sir!

But he is dead!

LAFFEMAS.

The Marquis de Saverny?

SAVERNY.

Yes, from a thrust in tierce, which burst the doublet,

Then carved its cruel way between the ribs

Through to the chest and to the liver, which,

As you well know, makes blood. The wound was fearful.

'Twas horrible to see

LAFFEMAS.

He died at once?

SAVERNY.

Almost. His agony was short. I watched

The spasm follow frenzy; tetanos

Then came, and after opisthotonos

There followed improstathonos.

LAFFEMAS.

The deuce!

SAVERNY.

So that I calculate 'tis false to say

The blood passes the jugular. Pequet

And learned men should be condemned when they

Dissect live dogs to study 'bout the lungs.

LAFFEMAS.

The poor marquis is dead.

SAVERNY.
 A thrust is fatal.
LAFFEMAS.
 You are a doctor, sir, of medicine?
SAVERNY.
 No.
LAFFEMAS.
 You have studied it?
SAVERNY.
 Somewhat.In Aristotle.
LAFFEMAS.
 You can talk it well!
SAVERNY.
 Faith! I've a most malicious sort of heart.
 I like destruction; find delight in evil;
 I love to kill! So that I thought I'd be
 A soldier or a doctor, sir, at twenty.
 But I hesitated long, and finally
 I chose the sword. It's not so sure, but twice
 As quick. There was a time, I will confess,
 I longed to be a poet or an actor,
 Or an exhibitor of bears—but then,
 I like dinner and supper every day.
 A plague upon the poetry and bears!
LAFFEMAS.
 With this hope in your mind you studied verse?
SAVERNY.
 A little bit, in Aristotle. Yes—
LAFFEMAS.
 The Marquis knew you?

SAVERNY.
He knew me as well
As a lieutenant knows an upstart soldier.
I belonged to Monsieur de Caussade first,
Who gave me to the Marquis' colonel. Poor
The present, but we do the best we can!
They made me officer—I'm worth as much
As any, and I wear a black mustache.
That is my history.
LAFFEMAS.
They sent you hereTo notify the uncle?
SAVERNY.
Yes; I came
With Brichanteau, the cousin, and the corpse.
He will be buried here—where, if he'd lived,
He would have had his wedding!
LAFFEMAS.
Tell me how
The old Marquis de Nangis bore the news.
SAVERNY.
With calmness, without tears.
LAFFEMAS.
He loved him though?
SAVERNY.
As much as we love life. Having no children
Of his own he had but this one passion—
His nephew, whom he dearly loved, although
They had not seen each other for five years.
[*In the background, the old* MARQUIS DE NANGIS *passes; white hair, pale countenance, arms folded across his breast,*

dress of the day of Henry IV.: deep mourning; the star and the ribbon of the order of the Holy Ghost. He walks slowly; nine guards in three rows follow; they are dressed in mourning, their halberds on their right shoulder, their muskets on their left; they keep within a short distance, stopping when he stops, and continuing when he continues.

LAFFEMAS (*watching him pass*).

Poor man!

[*He goes to the back and follows* THE MARQUIS *with his eyes.*

SAVERNY (*aside*).

My good old uncle!

[BRICHANTEAU *enters and goes to* SAVERNY.

SCENE II

The same. BRICHANTEAU

BRICHANTEAU.
   Ah! two words!
   [*Laughing.*] He's looking pretty well for a dead man!
SAVERNY (*low, indicating* THE MARQUIS, *who passes*).
   Why do you make me grieve him, Brichanteau?
   I think we might explain it to him now.
   Oh, let me try.
BRICHANTEAU.
   No; God forbid, my friend!
   His grief must be sincere; he must weep much.
   His woe is one good half of your disguise.
SAVERNY.
   Poor uncle!
BRICHANTEAU.
   He will find it out ere long.
SAVERNY.
   If sorrow has not killed him, then joy will.
   These shocks are dangerous to such old men.
BRICHANTEAU.
   It must be done!
SAVERNY.
   I cannot bear to hear
   Him laugh so bitterly, then weep; then keep
   So still! I hate to see him kiss that coffin.

BRICHANTEAU.

Yes—a fine coffin with no corpse in it!

SAVERNY.

But I am dead and bleeding in his heart.

The corpse lies there.

LAFFEMAS (*coming back*).

Alas, the poor old man!

His eyes show plainly how he's suffering!

BRICHANTEAU (*low to* Saverny).

Who is that surly-looking man in black?

SAVERNY (*with gesture of ignorance*).

Some friend who's living at the castle?

BRICHANTEAU (*low*).

Crows

Are also black and love the smell of death.

Keep silence more than ever. 'Tis a face

That's treacherous and evil; it would make

A madman prudent.

[THE MARQUIS DE NANGIS *re-enters; he is still absorbed in a deep reverie. He walks slowly, does not appear to notice any one, and seats himself upon a bank of turf.*

SCENE III

The same. MARQUIS DE NANGIS

LAFFEMAS (*approaching* The Marquis).

Marquis, we've lost much.

He was a rare man; would have comforted
　　Your old age. I mingle my tears with yours.
　　Young, handsome, good, naught more could be desired;
　　Obeying God, respecting women, strong;
　　Just in his actions, sensible in speech,
　　A perfect nobleman, whom all revere!
　　To die so young! Most cruel fate! Alas!
　　[THE MARQUIS *lets his head fall on his hands.*
SAVERNY (*low to* Brichanteau).
　　The devil take this funeral discourse!
　　These praises but augment the old man's grief.
　　Console him, you; Show him the other side.
BRICHANTEAU (*to* Laffemas).
　　You are mistaken, sir. I was in the
　　Same grade. A bad comrade, this Saverny—
　　A shiftless fellow, growing worse each day.
　　Courageous! Every man is brave at twenty;
　　His death is nothing much to boast about.
LAFFEMAS.
　　A duel! Surely, that is no great crime.
　　[*Banteringly to* BRICHANTEAU, *pointing to his sword.*
　　You are an officer?
BRICHANTEAU (*in the same tone, pointing to* LAFFEMAS's *wig*).
　　A magistrate?
SAVERNY (*low*).
　　Go on!
BRICHANTEAU.
　　He was capricious, thankless, and
　　A liar: not worth any real regret.

He went to church, but just to ogle girls.

He was a gallant, a mere libertine, A fool!

SAVERNY (*low*).

Good! good!

BRICHANTEAU.

Intractable and stubborn;

Rude to his officers. As to good looks,

He had lost his; he limped, had a large wen

Upon his eye; from blonde had turned to red,

And from round-shouldered had become hump-backed.

SAVERNY (*low*).

Enough!

BRICHANTEAU.

He gambled—every one knows that.

He would have staked his soul on dice. I'll wager

That cards had eaten up his property.

His fortune galloped faster every night.

SAVERNY (*low, pulling his sleeve*).

Enough! Good God! Your consolation is

Too strong.

LAFFEMAS.

To speak so ill of a dead friend!

Unpardonable!

BRICHANTEAU (*indicating* Saverny).

Ask this gentleman!

SAVERNY.

Oh, no; I beg to be excused!

LAFFEMAS (*affectionately, to the old* Marquis).

My lord,

We'll comfort you. We have his murderer,

And we will hang him. We have kept him safe.
His end is sure.
[*To* BRICHANTEAU *and* SAVERNY.
But can one understand
The Marquis? There are duels, we all know,
That cannot be avoided, but to fight
With any one named Didier—
SAVERNY (*aside*).
What? Didier?
[*The old* MARQUIS, *who has remained silent and motionless during all this scene, rises and goes out slowly on the side opposite where he came in. His guards follow him.*
LAFFEMAS (*wiping away a tear and following him with his eyes*).
In truth, his sorrow deeply touches me.
LACKEY (*running*).
My lord!
BRICHANTEAU.
Why can't you leave your master quiet?
LACKEY.
It is the burial of the young marquis!
What is the hour?
BRICHANTEAU.
You'll know it by-and-by.
LACKEY.
A few comedians have arrived here from
The city; they beg shelter for the night.
BRICHANTEAU.
The time's ill-chosen for comedians, but
The law of hospitality holds good.

Give them this barn.

[*Indicating a barn on the left.*

LACKEY (*holding a letter*).

A letter! 'Tis important!

[*Reading.*] For a Monsieur de Laffemas.

LAFFEMAS.

'Tis I!Give it to me!

BRICHANTEAU (*low to* SAVERNY, *who has remained thoughtful in a corner*).

Saverny, let us go!

Come and arrange things for your funeral!

[*Pulling him by the sleeve.*

What is it? Are you dreaming?

SAVERNY (*aside*).

Oh, Didier!

[*They go out.*

SCENE IV

LAFFEMAS (*alone*).

The seal of State! The great seal of red wax!
Come! this is business. Let me know at once!
[*Reading.*] "Sir Criminal Lieutenant: We make known
To you that Didier, the assassin of
The late Marquis Gaspard, has fled." My God!
That is unfortunate! "A woman is
With him, called Marion de Lorme. We beg
You to return as soon as possible."
Quick! Get me horses! I, who felt so sure!

Another matter spoiled for want of sense.
Outrageous! Of the two, not one! One, dead!
Escaped, the other! I will catch him, though!
[*He exits. Enter a troupe of strolling actors, men, women and children in character costumes. Among them are* MARION *and* DIDIER, *dressed as Spaniards.* DIDIER *wears a great felt hat and is covered with a cloak.*

SCENE V

The Comedians, MARION, DIDIER

A LACKEY (*conducting the Comedians to the barn*).
    This is your lodging. You're on the estate
    Of the Marquis de Nangis. Behave well,
    Try to be quiet, for some one is dead.
    The burial is to-morrow. Above all,
    Don't mix your songs with the funereal chants
    Which will be sung for him throughout the night.
GRACIEUX (*small and hump-backed*).
    We'll make less noise than do your hunting-dogs
    Who bark around the legs of all who pass!
LACKEY.
    Dogs are not actors, my good friend.
TAILLEBRAS (*to* Gracieux).
    Be still!
    You'll cause us to sleep in the open air!
    [LACKEY *exits.*

SCARAMOUCHE (*to* MARION *and* DIDIER, *who until now have remained quietly apart*).

    Come! let us talk. Now you belong to us.
    Why Monsieur fled with Madame on behind,
    If you are man and wife or lovers only,
    Escaping justice, or black sorcerers
    Who held Madame a prisoner, perhaps—
    Is not my business. What I want to know
    Is what you'll act. Chimènes are best for you,
    Black eyes.
    [MARION *makes a courtesy.*

DIDIER (*aside, indignant*).

    To hear that mountebank speak thus!

SCARAMOUCHE (*to* Didier).

    For you: if you should want a splendid part,
    We need a bully—a long-leggèd man,
    Tremendous strides, a thundering voice; and when
    Orgon is robbed of wife or niece, you kill
    The Moor and terminate the piece. Great part!
    High tragedy! 'Twill suit you splendidly.

DIDIER.

    Just as you please!

SCARAMOUCHE.

    Good! Don't say "you" to me!
    I like "thou"! [*With a profound obeisance.*
    Blusterer, hail!

DIDIER (*aside*).

    What fools!

SCARAMOUCHE (*to the other actors*).

    Now eat; Then we'll rehearse our parts.

[*All enter the barn except* MARION *and* DIDIER.

SCENE VI

MARION, DIDIER; *afterward* GRACIEUX, SAVERNY, *afterward*
LAFFEMAS

DIDIER (*with bitter laugh, after a long silence*).
   My Marion, have I dragged you low enough?
   You wished to follow me? My destiny
   Precipitates itself and crushes you,
      Bound to its wheel! What are we come to now?
   I told you so!
MARION (*trembling and clasping her hands*).
   Do you reproach me, love?
DIDIER.
   Oh, may I be accursed! Cursed first by Heaven,
   Then cursed 'mongst men: cursed throughout all my life;
   Cursed more than we are now, if a reproach
   Shall ever leave my lips for you! What matter
   Though all the earth abandon me, you're mine!
   You are my savior, refuge, all my hope!
   Who duped the jailer, filed my chains for me?
   Who came from heaven to follow me to hell?
   Who was a captive with the prisoner,
   An exile with the fugitive? Ah, who,
   Who else had heart so full of love and wit,
   Heart to sustain, console, deliver me?

Great, feeble woman, have you not saved me
From destiny, alas! and my own soul?
Had you not pity on my nature, crushed?
Have you not loved one whom all others hate?

MARION (*weeping*).
It is my joy to love you—be your slave.

DIDIER.
Leave me your eyes, dear; they enrapture me!
God willed, when placing soul within my flesh,
A demon and an angel should guide me.
Yet he was merciful; his love concealed
The demon, but the angel he revealed.

MARION.
You are my Didier, master, lord of me!

DIDIER.
Your husband, am I not?

MARION (*aside*).
Alas!

DIDIER.
What joy,
When we have left this country far behind,
To have you, call you wife as well as love!
You will be willing?—answer.

MARION.
I will beYour sister, and my brother you shall be!

DIDIER.
Oh, no! Refuse me not that ecstasy
Of knowing, in God's sight, you're mine alone!
You're safe to trust my love in everything.
The lover keeps you for the husband, pure!

MARION (*aside*).
　Alas!
DIDIER.
　If you knew how things torture me!
　To hear that actor talk, affront you thus!
　It is not least among our wretched woes
　To see you mixed with jugglers such as these,
　A chaste, exquisite flower 'mid this filth—
　You, 'mongst these women steeped in infamy!
MARION.
　Be prudent, Didier!
DIDIER.
　God! I struggled hard
　Against my anger! He said "thou" to you,
　When I, your love, your husband, hardly dare
　For fear of tarnishing that virgin brow—
MARION.
　Be pleasant with them; it means life to you,
　And me as well.
DIDIER.
　She's right. She's always right.
　Although each hour brings us increasing woe,
　You lavish on me love and joy and youth!
　How happens it these blessings come to me,
　When royal kingdoms were small pay for them—
　To me, who give but anguish in return?
　Heaven gave you—yes; but hell binds you to me.
　For us to merit this unequal fate,
　What good can I have done? What evil you?

MARION.
>My only blessings come from you, my love!

DIDIER.
>If you say that you think it, but it's wrong!
>Oh, yes, my star of destiny is bad.
>I know not whence I come, nor where I go.
>My whole horizon's dark. Love, hark to me!
>There's time yet; you can leave me and go back.
>Let me pursue the gloomy route alone.
>When all is ended and I'm tired out,
>The couch that's waiting will be cold—ice-cold,
>And narrow; there's not room enough for two.
>Go back!

MARION.
>That couch, dark, and mysterious,
>I'll share it with you; that at least is mine.

DIDIER.
>Will you not listen? Can't you understand?
>You're tempting Providence to cling to me!
>The years of anguish, love, may be so long
>Your sweet eyes may grow sightless, just from tears.
>[MARION *lets her head fall on her hands.*

DIDIER.
>I swear I draw the picture none too strong.
>Your future frightens me. I pity you!
>Go back!

MARION (*bursting into tears*).
>It were more kind to kill me, Didier,
>Than to talk thus! [*Weeping.*] O God!

DIDIER (*taking her in his arms*).

    My darling, hush!

    So many tears! I'd shed my blood for one.

    Do what you will! Come, be my destiny,

    My glory, life, my virtue, and my love!

    Answer me now. I speak! Sweet, do you hear?

    [*He seats her on a bank of turf.*

MARION (*withdrawing herself from his arms*).

    You've hurt me!

DIDIER (*kneeling to her*).

    I, who'd gladly die for her!

MARION (*smiling through her tears*).

    You made me cry, you cruel man!

DIDIER.

    My beauty!

    [*Sits on the bank beside her.*

    Just one sweet kiss upon your forehead, pure

    As is our love!

    [*He kisses her forehead. They look at each other with ecstasy.*

    Yes, look at me! Look thus,

    Look harder; look until we die of looking!

GRACIEUX (*entering*).

    Dona Chimène is wanted in the barn.

    [MARION *rises hastily from* DIDIER'S *side. At the same time that* GRACIEUX *enters,* SAVERNY *comes in; he stands in the background and looks attentively at* MARION *without seeing Didier, who remains sitting on the bank and is hidden by a bush.*

SAVERNY (*back, without being seen, aside*).

    Faith, it is Marion! What brings her here?

[*Laughing.*] Chimène!
GRACIEUX (*to* Didier, *who is about to follow* MARION).
   Oh, no! stay there, my jealous friend,
   I want to tease you!
DIDIER.
   Devil take you!
MARION (*low to* Didier).
   Hush!
   Restrain yourself.
   [Didier *re-seats himself; she enters the barn.*
SAVERNY (*still back, aside*).
   What makes her roam the country in this fashion?
   Can he be the gallant who succored me?
   Who saved my life? Didier! It is indeed!
LAFFEMAS (*enters in traveling costume, and salutes* Saverny).
   I take my leave, sir!
SAVERNY (*bowing*).
   You are going away?
   [*He laughs.*
LAFFEMAS.
   What makes you laugh?
SAVERNY.
   A very silly thing.
   I'll tell you. Guess whom I have recognized
   Among those jugglers who have just arrived.
LAFFEMAS.
   Among those jugglers?
SAVERNY (*laughing still more*).
   Yes. Marion de Lorme!

LAFFEMAS (*with a start*).

Marion de Lorme!

DIDIER (*who has been looking at them fixedly all the time*).

Hein? [*He half rises from the bank.*

SAVERNY (*still laughing*).

I would like to send

That news to Paris. Are you going there?

LAFFEMAS.

I am, and I will spread the news, trust me!

But are you sure you recognize her?

SAVERNY.

Sure?

Hurrah for France! We know our Marion.

[*Feeling in his pocket.*

I think I have her portrait—tender pledge

Of love! She had it done by the King's painter.

[*Giving* Laffemas *a locket.*

Look and compare them.

[*Indicating the barn door.*

See her, through that door,

In Spanish costume, with green petticoat.

LAFFEMAS (*looking from the locket to the barn*).

'Tis she—Marion de Lorme! [*Aside.*] I have him now!

[*To* SAVERNY.] She must have a companion 'mongst these men.

SAVERNY.

It's likely. Such fair ladies are not prudes,

And seldom travel round the world alone.

LAFFEMAS (*aside*).

I'll guard this door. It will go hard, indeed,

If I can't capture that false actor here.
He's taken now—no doubt of that! [*Goes out.*
SAVERNY (*watches the exit of* Laffemas: *aside*).
I thinkI've done a foolish thing.
[*Taking* GRACIEUX *aside, who all this time has stood in a corner gesticulating and running over his lines: in a whisper.*
Who is that lady
Sitting within the shadow there?
[*Indicating the door of the barn.*
GRACIEUX.
Chimène?
[*Solemnly.*] My lord, I do not know her name. Ask him,
This lord, her noble friend.
[*Exits on the side of the park.*

SCENE VII

Didier, Saverny
SAVERNY (*turning toward* Didier).
This gentleman?
Tell me— 'Tis strange how hard he looks at me!
Upon my soul, 'tis he! My man! [*Loud to* DIDIER.] If you
Were not in prison, I should say that you
Resemble a—
DIDIER.
And if you were not dead, I'd say
That you had the exact appearance of—
His blood be on his head!—a man whom two
Short words of mine put in a tomb.

SAVERNY.

Hush! You Are Didier!

DIDIER.

Marquis Gaspard, you!

SAVERNY.

'Twas you

Who were somewhere, a certain night! 'Tis you

To whom I owe my life!

[*He opens his arms.* DIDIER *draws back.*

DIDIER.

Excuse surprise!

I felt so sure I took it back.

SAVERNY.

Not so!

You saved me—did not kill me! Let me know

What I can do for you. Do you desire

A second—brother—a lieutenant? Speak!

What will you have—my blood, my wealth, my soul?

DIDIER.

Not any of those things. That portrait there!

[SAVERNY *gives him the portrait; he looks at it, speaking with bitterness.*

Yes, there's her brow, her black eyes, her white neck;

Above all, there's her candid glance! How like!

SAVERNY.

You think so?

DIDIER.

This was made for you, you say?

SAVERNY (*bowing, and making an affirmative sign*).

It was! But now 'tis you whom she prefers,

You whom she loves and chooses 'mongst us all.
You are a happy man.
DIDIER (*with loud and mocking laugh*).
Yes! Am I not?
SAVERNY.
Accept my compliments; she's a good girl,
And loves no one but men of family.
Of such a mistress one can well be proud!
It's honorable, and it gives one style.'
Tis in good taste. If men ask who you are
They say, "Beloved of Marion de Lorme."
[DIDIER *gives him back the portrait; he refuses it.*
No, keep the portrait; since the lady's yours,
It should belong to you. Keep it, I pray.
DIDIER.
I thank you! [*Puts it in his breast.*
SAVERNY.
She is charming in that dress.
So you are my successor! One might say,
As King Louis succeeded Pharamond.
The Brissacs, both of them, supplanted me.
[*Laughing.*] Then, yes, the Cardinal himself came next,
Then little D'Effiat, then the three Sainte-Mesmes,
The four Argenteans! In her heart you'll find
The best society. [*Laughing.*] A little numerous.
DIDIER (*aside*).
My God!
SAVERNY.
Tell me about it some time. Now,
To be quite frank with you, I pass for dead,

And in the morning shall be buried. You
Must have escaped police and seneschals.
Your Marion can manage everything!
You joined a strolling company by chance;
What a delightful history!

DIDIER.

Yes, trueIt is a history!

SAVERNY.

To get you out
She probably made love to all the jailers.

DIDIER (*in a voice of thunder*).

Do you think that?

SAVERNY.

You are not jealous—what?
Oh, joke incredible!—of Marion!
A man jealous of Marion! The poor child!
Don't go and scold her!

DIDIER.

Have no fear. [*Aside.*] The angel—
It was a demon! Oh, my God!

[*Enter* LAFFEMAS *and* GRACIEUX. DIDIER *goes out;* SAVERNY *follows him.*

SCENE VIII

LAFFEMAS, GRACIEUX

GRACIEUX (*to* Laffemas).
  My lord,
  I do not understand you!
  [*Aside.*] Humph! A costume
  Of Alcaid and a figure of police;
  Small eyes, adorned with big eyebrows! I think
  He plays the part of Alguazil in this
  Locality.
LAFFEMAS (*pulling out his purse*).
  My friend!
GRACIEUX (*drawing near, low to* Laffemas).
  My lord—I see!
  Chimène has interested you. You wish
  To know—
LAFFEMAS (*low, smiling*).
  Who is her Roderick?
GRACIEUX.
  You meanHer lover?
LAFFEMAS.
  Yes!
GRACIEUX.
  Who groans beneath her spell?
LAFFEMAS (*impatiently*).
  There's one?

GRACIEUX.

Of course!

LAFFEMAS (*approaching him eagerly*).

Then show him to me, quick!

GRACIEUX (*with profound obeisance*).

It's I, my lord. I'm mad about her!

LAFFEMAS.

You!

[LAFFEMAS, *disappointed, turns away with annoyance; then he comes back and shakes his purse in* GRACIEUX'S *eyes and ears.*

Know you the sound of ducats?

GRACIEUX.

Heavenly tones!

LAFFEMAS (*aside*).

I've got my Didier![*To* GRACIEUX.] Do you see this purse?

GRACIEUX.

How much!

LAFFEMAS.

Gold ducats—twenty!

GRACIEUX.

Humph!

LAFFEMAS (*jingling the gold in his face*).

Will you?

GRACIEUX (*grabbing the purse from him*).

Most certainly!

[*With theatrical tone to* LAFFEMAS, *who listens anxiously.*

My lord, if your back bore
Just in the center a great hump, as big
As is your belly, and if those two bags

Were filled with louis, sequins, and doubloons,
In that case—
LAFFEMAS (*eagerly*).
Well, what would you do?
GRACIEUX (*putting the purse into his pocket*).
I'd take
The whole of it, and I would say—
[*With profound obeisance.*
I thank you;
You are a gentleman!
LAFFEMAS (*aside, furious*).
Plague on the monkey!
GRACIEUX (*aside, laughing*).
The devil take the cat!
LAFFEMAS (*aside*).
They have agreed
On what to do, if any one suspects.
'Tis a conspiracy. They'll all be dumb;
Accursed gypsy devils!
[*To* GRACIEUX *who is going away.*
Give me back My purse!
GRACIEUX (*turning around, with tragic tone*).
What do you take me for, my lord?
What will the world think of us, pray, if you
Propose and I agree to anything
So infamous as sell for gold a life,
My soul? [*Turns to go.*
LAFFEMAS.
That's as you please; but give me back My money!

GRACIEUX.
No, I keep my honor, sir, And we have no accounts to settle.
[*He salutes him and re-enters barn.*]

SCENE IX

LAFFEMAS (*alone*).
Humph!
The wretched juggler! Pride in such base souls!
If you some day should fall into my hands
Unoccupied with better sort of game—
But this will not find Didier! Now, I can't
Take all this crowd and put them to the torture.
This is worse work than hunting needles in
A haystack. Faith! a chemist's crucible
Bewitched I ought to have, which, eating up
The lead and copper, would reveal at last
The golden ingot hid by much alloy.
Go to the Cardinal without my prize?
[*Striking his brow.*
That's it! The clever thought! Oh, joy! He's mine!
[*Calling through the barn door.*
Ho, gentlemen, comedians! one word, please.
[*The actors crowd out of the barn.*

SCENE X

The same. Comedians, among them MARION *and* DIDIER; *afterward* SAVERNY, *afterward* MARQUIS DE NANGIS

SCARAMOUCHE (*to* Laffemas).
   What do you want with us?
LAFFEMAS.
   Without preamble:
   My lord the Cardinal commissioned me
   To find good actors, if there may be such
   Within the provinces, to act the plays
   Which he constructs in hours of leisure when
   Allowed by State affairs. In spite of care
   And earnest thought, his theater declines,
   And is no credit to a cardinal-duke.
   [*All the actors press eagerly forward. Saverny enters, and watches the scene with curiosity.*
GRACIEUX (*aside, counting his money*).
   Twelve only! He said twenty. The old scamp!
   He's robbed me!
LAFFEMAS.
   Let each one repeat some scene,
   That I may know your talents and may choose.
   [*Aside.*] If he gets out of that, this Didier's sharp.
   [*Aloud.*] Are you all here?
   [MARION *stealthily approaches* DIDIER *and tries to lead him off.*

GRACIEUX (*going up to them*).

　Come with the others—you!

MARION.

　Oh, heaven!

[DIDIER *leaves her and joins the actors; she follows him.*

GRACIEUX.

　You're in luck to be with us.

　To have new clothes, get every day a feast,

　To speak the Cardinal's verses every night,

　A happy lot!

[*All the actors take their places before* LAFFEMAS. MARION *and* DIDIER *among them.* DIDIER *does not look at* MARION; *his eyes are bent on the ground; his arms are folded underneath his cloak.* MARION *watches him anxiously.*

GRACIEUX (*at head of troupe, aside*).

　Who would have thought this crow

　Recruited actors for the Cardinal?

LAFFEMAS (*to* Gracieux).

　First you. What do you play?

GRACIEUX (*with a low bow and a pirouette which shows off his hump*).

　I'm called the Sylph

　Among the troupe. This piece I know the best.

　[*He sings.*

　"On the bald heads of magistrates,

　Enormous wigs are spread.

　Out of that fleece, in due time, come

　Chains, gallows, tortures dread.

　Whenever one called president

　Shall shake his bigger head.

"Let any barber, strolling fool,
Wash, powder, and pomade
The hair which bald heads steal from beards,
Let them be combed and frayed
In shape of a right gorgeous wig—
Your magistrate is made.
"The lawyer is a sea of words
Hurled wildly at the bench.
A killing kind of mixing up
Of Latin and bad French—"

LAFFEMAS (*interrupting him*).
   You sing so false, you'd make an eagle sick.
   Be still!

GRACIEUX (*laughing*).
   I may sing false—the song is true!

LAFFEMAS (*to* Scaramouche).
   It's your turn now.

SCARAMOUCHE (*bowing*).
   I'm Scaramouche, my lord!
   "The Lady of Honor," sir, I open thus.
   [*Declaiming.*
   "'Naught is so fine,' said once a Queen of Spain,
   'As bishop at the altar, soldier in
   The field, unless it is a girl in bed,
   Or robber on the gallows—'"

[LAFFEMAS *interrupts* SCARAMOUCHE *with a gesture and signs to* TAILLEBRAS *to speak.* TAILLEBRAS *makes a profound obeisance, then draws himself up.*

TAILLEBRAS (*with emphasis*).
   As for me,

Sir, I am Taillebras. From Thibet, sir,
I come; I've punished the great Khan, I've captured
The Mogul—

LAFFEMAS.

Choose something else—
[*Low to* Saverny, *who stands beside him.*
A beauty,
Eh, this Marion!

TAILLEBRAS.

It is one of our best.
If you prefer, I will be Charlemagne,
The Emperor of the West.
[*Declaiming with emphasis.*
"Strange destiny!
O Heaven, I appeal to you! Bear witness
Unto my woe. I must despoil myself,
Surrender my beloved one to another.
I must endow my rival, fill his heart
With joy, while my poor stomach stings with grief.
Thus, birds, you can no more perch in the woods;
Thus, flies, you can no more buzz in the fields;
Thus, sheep, you can no longer wear your wool;
Thus, bulls, you can no longer raze the plains."

LAFFEMAS.

Good![*To* SAVERNY.] Listen, the fine verses! "Bradamante"
By Garnier; what a poet![*To* MARION.] 'Tis your turn,
My beauty. First, your name.

MARION (*trembling*).

I am Chimène!

LAFFEMAS.

Indeed! Chimène? Then you must have a lover.

He has killed a man in duel—

MARION (*terrified*).

Oh, heaven!

LAFFEMAS (*maliciously*).

I've a good memory. If one escapes—

MARION (*aside*).

Great heaven!

LAFFEMAS.

Come! Now let us hear your scene

MARION (*half turned toward* DIDIER).

"Since to arrest you in this fatal course
Your life and honor are of no avail,
If ever I have loved you, Roderick,
Defend yourself to save me from Don Sancho.
Fight valiantly against the fearful fate
Which must surrender me to one I hate.
Shall I say more? Go; your defense shall be
Your right to force my duty, seal my lips!
If love for me still in your brave heart lies,
Go win this combat, for Chimène is prize."

[LAFFEMAS *rises gallantly and kisses her hand.* MARION *is pale; she looks at* DIDIER, *who remains motionless with eyes on the ground.*

LAFFEMAS.

No voice but yours could take so firm a hold
Upon the secret fibers of our heart.
You are adorable.

[*To* SAVERNY.] You can't deny

Corneille is not worth Garnier, after all.
'Tis true, his verses have a finer ring
Since he's belonged unto the Cardinal-Duke.
[*To* MARION.] What a complexion! What fine eyes! Good God!
This is no place for you! You're buried here.
Sit down!
[*He sits and makes sign to* MARION *to sit beside him; she draws back.*]

MARION (*low to* Didier, *with anguish*).
For God's sake, let me stay with you!

LAFFEMAS (*smiling*).
Come sit by me, I say!
[DIDIER *repulses* MARION, *who staggers terrified to the bench where* Laffemas *sits, and falls upon it.*]

MARION (*aside*).
'Tis horrible!

LAFFEMAS (*smiling at Marion, with an air of reproach*).
At last!
[*To* DIDIER.] Now, sir, your turn. What is your name?

DIDIER (*with gravity*).
My name is Didier!

MARION, LAFFEMAS, SAVERNY.
Didier!

DIDIER (*to* LAFFEMAS, *who laughs triumphantly*).
Yes, you can
Send all of them away. You've got your prey.
Your prisoner himself takes up his chain.
This joy has cost you a great deal of work.

MARION (*running to him*).
Didier!

DIDIER (*with a freezing look*).
   Don't try to hinder me this time,
   Madame!
   [*She starts back and falls crushed upon the bank: to* LAFFEMAS.
   I've watched you creeping close to me,
   You demon! In your eyes I've seen that glare
   Of hell fire which illuminates your soul.
   I might have 'scaped your trap—a useless thing;
   But to see cunning wasted thus grieved me.
   Take me, and get well paid for treachery.
LAFFEMAS (*with concentrated rage, trying to laugh*).
   You are not a comedian, it would seem!
DIDIER.
   It's you who played the comedy.
LAFFEMAS.
   Not well.
   But with the Cardinal I'll write a play.
   It is a tragedy: you have a part.
   [MARION *screams with horror.* DIDIER *turns from her with contempt.*
   Don't turn your head in such a lordly way.
   We will admire your acting, never fear!
   Come, recommend your soul to God, my friend.
MARION.
   Ah, God!
   [*At this moment* MARQUIS DE NANGIS *passes across the back of the stage, in the same attitude, with his escort of Halberdiers.* MARION'S *cry arrests him; pale and silent he turns to the characters.*

LAFFEMAS (*to* Marquis de Nangis).
   Marquis, I claim your aid. Good news!
   Lend me your escort. The murderer escaped
   Our vigilance, but we've recaptured him.
MARION (*throwing herself at* Laffemas's *feet*).
   Oh, pity for him!
LAFFEMAS (*with gallantry*).
   At my feet, madame!
   'Tis I should kneel at yours.
MARION (*on her knees, clasping her hands*).
   My lord the judge,
   Have mercy upon others, if some day
   You hope a jealous judge, more powerful
   Than you are, will be merciful to you!
LAFFEMAS (*smiling*).
   You're preaching us a sermon, I believe!
   Ah, madame, reign at balls and shine at fêtes,
   But do not preach us sermons. For your sake,
   I would do anything; but he has killed—
   It is a murder.
DIDIER (*to* MARION).
   Rise! [MARION *rises, trembling.*
   You lie! it was a duel.
LAFFEMAS.
   Sir!
DIDIER.
   I say, you lie!
LAFFEMAS.
   Have done!
   [*To* MARION.] Blood calls

For blood; this rigor troubles me— I wish—
But he has killed—killed whom?
The young marquis,
Gaspard de Saverny,
[*Indicating* MARQUIS DE NANGIS.
Nephew to him,
That worthy old man there. A rare young lord;
The greatest loss for France and for the King.
Were he not dead, I do not say that I—
My heart is not of stone, and if—

SAVERNY (*taking a step forward*).
The man
You think is dead is living. I am he!
[*General astonishment.*

LAFFEMAS (*starting*).
Gaspard de Saverny! A miracle!
There is his coffin.

SAVERNY (*tearing off his false mustache, his plaster, and black wig*).
But he is not dead!
Who recognizes me?

MARQUIS DE NANGIS (*as if awakening from a dream, starts, and with a great cry throws himself into his nephew's arms*).
Gaspard! My nephew!
It is my child! [*They remain locked in each other's arms.*

MARION (*falling upon her knees and lifting her eyes to heaven*).
Didier is saved! Praise God!

DIDIER (*coldly, to* Saverny).
What is the use? I wished to die.

MARION (*still on her knees*).

   Kind God, You have protected him!

DIDIER (*continuing, without listening to her*).

   How otherwise

   Could he have caught me in his trap? Think you

   My spur could not have crushed the spider's web

   Which he had made to catch a gnat? Henceforth

   I ask no other boon than death. This is

   No friendly gift from you, who owe me life!

MARION.

   What does he say? You must live—

LAFFEMAS.

   All's not over.

   Is it certain that this is the Marquis?

MARION.

   It is.

LAFFEMAS.

   We must have proof of it at once.

MARION (*indicating* MARQUIS DE NANGIS, *who is still holding* SAVERNY *in his arms*).

   Look at that old man, how he smiles and weeps!

LAFFEMAS.

   Is that Gaspard de Saverny?

MARION.

   What heart

   Can question such a close embrace?

MARQUIS DE NANGIS (*turning around*).

   You askIf it is he—Gaspard, my son, my soul?

   [*To* MARION.] Did he not ask if it was he, madame?

LAFFEMAS (*to* MARQUIS DE NANGIS).

Then you affirm that this man is your nephew?

He is Gaspard de Saverny?

MARQUIS DE NANGIS (*with intensity*).

I do!

LAFFEMAS.

According to the law I do arrest

Gaspard de Saverny, in the King's name.

Your sword!

[*Surprise and consternation among the characters.*

MARQUIS DE NANGIS.

My son!

MARION.

Oh, Heaven!

DIDIER.

Another head!

Yes, two were needed. 'Tis the least, to bring

This Roman Cæsar one head in each hand.

MARQUIS DE NANGIS.

Speak! By what right—

LAFFEMAS.

Ask my lord cardinal.

All who survive a duel fall beneath

The ordinance. Give me your sword.

DIDIER (*looking at* Saverny).

Rash man!

SAVERNY (*drawing his sword and presenting it to* LAFFEMAS).

'Tis here!

MARQUIS DE NANGIS (*stopping him*).

A moment! None is master here

Save me! I mete out justice high and low.
Our sire the King would be no more than guest.
[*To* SAVERNY.] Give up your sword to none but me.
[SAVERNY *hands him his sword, and clasps him in his arms.*

LAFFEMAS.
In truth,
That is a feudal right quite out of date.
The Cardinal might blame me for it, but
I would not willingly annoy you—

DIDIER.
Wretch!

LAFFEMAS (*bowing to* MARQUIS DE NANGIS).
So I consent. You can return the favor
By loaning me your guard and prison, sir.

MARQUIS DE NANGIS (*to his Guards*).
Not so! Your sires were vassals to my sires.
I forbid any one to stir a step.

LAFFEMAS (*with voice of thunder*).
My masters, hark to me: I am the judge
Of the secret tribunal, Criminal-
Lieutenant to the Cardinal. Conduct
These men to prison. Four of you mount guard
Before each door. You're all responsible.
It would be rash to disobey when I command
You to go here or there or do a deed.
If any hesitate, it is because
His head annoys him.

[*The Guards, terrified, drag the two prisoners off in silence,* MARQUIS DE NANGIS *turns away indignant and buries his face in his hands.*

MARION.
　All is lost!
　[*To* LAFFEMAS.] Have pity!
　If in your heart—
LAFFEMAS (*low to* MARION).
　If you will come to-night,
　I'll tell you something—
MARION (*aside*).
　What is it he wants?
　His smiles are terrible. He has a gloomy,
　Treacherous soul.
　[*Turning with desperation to* Didier.
　Didier!
DIDIER (*coldly*).
　Farewell, madame!
MARION (*shuddering at the tone of his voice*).
　What have I done? Oh, miserable woman!
　[*She sinks upon the bank.*
DIDIER.
　Miserable! Yes!
SAVERNY (*embraces* MARQUIS DE NANGIS, *then turns to* Laffemas).
　Is your pay doubled
　When you bring two heads?
LACKEY (*entering, to* Marquis de Nangis).
　My lord,
　The funeral preparations for the Marquis
　Are now completed. I am sent to you
　To know what hour and day the ceremony
　Will be performed.

LAFFEMAS.
Come back one month from now.
[*The Guards lead off* Didier *and* Saverny.

ACT IV.

THE KING

SCENE.—*Chambord. The guard-room in the Castle of Chambord*

SCENE I

Duke de Bellegarde, *rich court costume covered with embroidery and lace, the order of the Holy Ghost around his neck, and the star upon his cloak.* Marquis de Nangis, *in deep mourning and followed by his escort of Guards. Both cross the back of the hall*

DUKE DE BELLEGARDE.
Condemned?
MARQUIS DE NANGIS.
Condemned!
DUKE DE BELLEGARDE.
E'en so! The King can pardon.
It is his kingly right and royal duty.

Have no more fear. In heart as well as name
He's son of Henry IV.
MARQUIS DE NANGIS.
I was his comrade.
DUKE DE BELLEGARDE.
Indeed, we spoiled full many a coat of armor
For the proud sire! Now go unto the son,
Show him your gray hairs, and in lieu of prayer
Cry out "Ventre Saint Gris!" Let Richelieu
Himself give better reason! Hide here now.
[*He opens a side door.*
He's coming soon. Do you know, to be frank,
Your costume's of a style to make one laugh.
MARQUIS DE NANGIS.
Laugh at my mourning?
DUKE DE BELLEGARDE.
Ah, these coxcombs here!
Old friend, stay there; you'll not have long to wait.
I will dispose him 'gainst the Cardinal.
I'll stamp upon the ground for signal; then
Come out.
MARQUIS DE NANGIS (*grasping his hand*).
May God repay you!
DUKE DE BELLEGARDE (*to a* MUSKETEER *who walks up and down in front of a small gilt door*).
Monsieur, pray,
What does the King?
MUSKETEER.
He's working, my lord duke!
[*Lowering his voice.*

A man in black is with him.
DUKE DE BELLEGARDE (*aside*).
   At this moment
He is singing a death-warrant, I believe.
[*To the old* Marquis, *grasping his hand.*
Be brave!
[*He conducts him to a neighboring gallery.*
While waiting for the signal, look
At these new ceilings, they're by Primatice.
[*Both go out.* MARION, *in deep mourning, enters through the great door in the back, which opens on a staircase.*

SCENE II

MARION, *the Guards*

HALBERDIER (*to* Marion).
   Madame, you cannot enter!
MARION (*advancing*).
   Sir!
HALBERDIER (*placing his halberd against the door*).
   I say,
   No entrance!
MARION (*with contempt*).
   Here you turn your lance against
   A woman. Elsewhere, 'tis in her defense.
MUSKETEER (*laughing, to* HALBERDIER).
   Well said!

MARION (*firmly*).
  I must immediately have audience
  With the Duke de Bellegarde.
HALBERDIER (*lowering his halberd, aside*).
  Ah, these gallants!
MUSKETEER.
  Enter, madame.
  [*She enters with determined step.*
HALBERDIER (*aside, watching her from the corner of his eye*).
  Well, the old duke is not
  As feeble as he looks. This rendezvous
  Would have cost him a sojourn in the Louvre,
  In former times.
MUSKETEER (*making sign to* HALBERDIER *to keep still*).
  The door is open.
  [*The little gilt door is opened.* M. DE LAFFEMAS *comes out, holding in his hand a parchment to which a red seal hangs by strands of silk.*

SCENE III

MARION, LAFFEMAS: *gesture of surprise from both.* MARION *turns away from him with horror*

LAFFEMAS (*low, advancing slowly toward* MARION).
  You!
  What is your errand here?

MARION.
   What's yours?
LAFFEMAS (*unrolls the parchment and spreads it out before her eyes*).
   Signed by The King!
MARION (*glances at it, then buries her face in her hands*).
   Good God!
LAFFEMAS (*speaking in her ear*).
   Will you?
[MARION *shivers and looks him in the face; he fixes his eyes on hers: lowering his voice.*
   Wilt thou?
MARION (*pushing him away*).
   Away!
   Foul tempter!
LAFFEMAS (*straightening himself up, sneeringly*).
   You will not!
MARION.
   I have no fear!
   The King can pardon: 'tis the King who reigns.
LAFFEMAS.
   Go try him. See what his good will is worth!
[*He turns away, then turns back: folds his arms and whispers to her.*
   Beware of waiting until I refuse!
[*Exits.* Duke de Bellegarde *enters.*

SCENE IV

Marion, Duke de Bellegarde

MARION (*going toward* Duke de Bellegarde).
Here you are captain, my lord duke.
DUKE DE BELLEGARDE.
'Tis you, My beauty! [*Bowing.*Speak! What does my queen desire?
MARION.
To see the King.
DUKE DE BELLEGARDE.
When?
MARION.
Now!
DUKE DE BELLEGARDE.
This is short notice!
Why?
MARION.
For something!
DUKE DE BELLEGARDE (*bursting into a laugh*).
We will send for him!
How she goes on!
MARION.
Then you refuse me?
DUKE DE BELLEGARDE.
Nay! Am I not yours? Have we refused each other
Anything?

MARION.

    That's very well, my lord! When shall I see the King?

DUKE DE BELLEGARDE.

    After the Duke.
    I promise you shall see him when he passes
    Through this hall. But while waiting, talk with me!
    Ah, little woman, are we good? In black?
    Lady-in-waiting you might be. You used
    To laugh so much.

MARION.

    I don't laugh now.

DUKE DE BELLEGARDE.

    Indeed! I think she's weeping! Marion! You?

MARION (*wiping her eyes: with firm tone*).

    My lord, I want to see his Majesty at once!

DUKE DE BELLEGARDE.

    For what?

MARION.

    Just Heaven! For—

DUKE DE BELLEGARDE.

    Is it against The Cardinal?

MARION.

    It is!

DUKE DE BELLEGARDE (*opening the gallery for her*).

    Please enter here.
    I put the discontented all in there;
    Do not come out before the signal, please.
    [*Marion enters; he shuts door.*
    I would have run the risk for my old friend.
    It costs no more to do it for them both.

[*The hall is gradually filled with Courtiers; they talk together.* DUKE DE BELLEGARDE *goes from one to the other.* L'ANGELY *enters.*

SCENE V

The same. DUKE DE BEAUPRÉAU, LAFFEMAS, VISCOUNT DE ROHAN, COUNT DE CHARNACÉ, ABBÉ DE GONDI, *and other courtiers*

DUKE DE BELLEGARDE (*to* Duke de Beaupréau).
  Good-morning, Duke!
DUKE DE BEAUPRÉAU.
  Good-morning!
DUKE DE BELLEGARDE.
  Any news?
DUKE DE BEAUPRÉAU.
  There's talk of a new cardinal.
DUKE DE BELLEGARDE.
  Which one? The Archbishop of Arle?
DUKE DE BEAUPRÉAU.
  No! Bishop of Autun.
  All Paris thinks he has obtained the hat.
ABBÉ DE GONDI.
  'Tis his by right. He was commander of
  Artillery at the siege of La Rochelle.
DUKE DE BELLEGARDE.
  That's true!

L'ANGELY.

The Holy See has my approval.

This one will be a cardinal according

To the canons.

ABBÉ DE GONDI (*laughing*).

L'Angely—the fool!

L'ANGELY (*bowing*).

My lord knows all my names.

[LAFFEMAS *enters; all the Courtiers vie with each other in paying court to him and surrounding him.* DUKE DE BELLEGARDE *watches them with vexation.*

DUKE DE BELLEGARDE (*to* L'ANGELY).

Fool, who's that man

Who wears the ermine cloak?

L'ANGELY.

Whom every oneIs paying court to?

DUKE DE BELLEGARDE.

Yes. I know him not.

Is he a follower of Monsieur d'Orleans?

L'ANGELY.

They would not fawn on him so much.

DUKE DE BELLEGARDE (*watching* LAFFEMAS, *who struts about*).

What airs!

As if he were grandee of Spain!

L'ANGELY (*low*).

It is Sir Laffemas, intendant of Champagne,

Lieutenant-Criminal—

DUKE DE BELLEGARDE (*low*).

Infernal, say!

He's called the Cardinal's executioner?
L'ANGELY (*still low*).
The same.
DUKE DE BELLEGARDE.
That man at Court!
L'ANGELY.
Why not? One extra
Tiger-cat in the menagerie!
Shall I present him?
DUKE DE BELLEGARDE (*haughtily*).
Peace, you fool!
L'ANGELY.
I think I'd cultivate him if I were a lord.
Be friendly! Unto each man comes his day.
If he takes not your hand, he may your head.
[*He seeks* LAFFEMAS, *presents him to* DUKE DE BELLEGARDE, *who bows with ill-concealed displeasure.*
LAFFEMAS (*bowing*).
Sir Duke!
DUKE DE BELLEGARDE.
Sir, I am charmed—[*Aside.*] Upon my life,
We're fallen low, Monsieur de Richelieu!
[Laffemas *walks away.*
VISCOUNT DE ROHAN (*bursting into laughter among a group of Courtiers in the back of the hall*).
Delightful!
L'ANGELY.
What?
VISCOUNT DE ROHAN.
That Marion is here.

L'ANGELY.

Here—Marion?

VISCOUNT DE ROHAN.

We were just saying this:

"Chaste Louis's guest is Marion." How rich!

L'ANGELY.

A charming piece of wit, indeed, my lord!

DUKE DE BELLEGARDE (*to* COUNT DE CHARNACÉ).

Sir wolf-hunter, have you found any prey?

Is hunting good?

COUNT DE CHARNACÉ.

There's nothing! Yesterday
I had great expectations, for three peasants
Had been devoured by wolves. At first I thought
We would find several at Chambord. I beat
The woods, but not a wolf, nor trace of one!

[*To* L'ANGELY.] Fool, know you anything that's gay?

L'ANGELY.

Nothing,
My lord, except two men will soon be hanged
At Beaugency for dueling.

ABBÉ DE GONDI.

So little, Bah! [*The small gilt door is opened.*

AN USHER.

The King!

[THE KING *enters; he is in black, his eyes are cast down. The order of the Holy Ghost is on his doublet and his cloak. Hat on his head. The Courtiers all uncover and range themselves, silently, in two rows. The Guards lower their pikes and present muskets.*

SCENE VI

The same. The King. THE KING *enters slowly, passes through the crowd of Courtiers, without lifting his head, stops at front of stage, and stands for several instants absorbed and silent. The Courtiers retire to the back of the hall*

THE KING.
   All things move on from bad to worse. Yes, all!
   [*To Courtiers, nodding his head.*
   God keep you, gentlemen!
   [*He throws himself into a large armchair and sighs profoundly.*
   I have slept ill!
   [*To* DUKE DE BELLEGARDE.
   My lord!
DUKE DE BELLEGARDE (*advancing with three profound salutations*).
   The time for sleeping, sire, is past.
THE KING (*eagerly*).
   True, Duke! The State is rushing to destruction
   With giant strides!
DUKE DE BELLEGARDE.
   'Tis guided by a handBoth strong and wise.
THE KING.
   He bears a heavy burden,
   Our good lord cardinal!
DUKE DE BELLEGARDE.
   Sire!

THE KING.
>He is old.
>I ought to spare him, but I have enough
>To do with living, without reigning!

DUKE DE BELLEGARDE.
>Sire, The Cardinal's not old!

THE KING.
>Pray, tell me frankly—
>No one is watching or is listening here—
>What do you think of him?

DUKE DE BELLEGARDE.
>Of whom, sire?

THE KING.
>Him!

DUKE DE BELLEGARDE.
>His Eminence?

THE KING.
>Of course!

DUKE DE BELLEGARDE.
>My dazzled eyes Can hardly fix themselves—

THE KING.
>Is that your frankness?
>There is no cardinal here, nor red, nor gray!
>No spies! Speak! Why are you afraid? The King
>Wants your opinion of the Cardinal.

DUKE DE BELLEGARDE.
>Entirely frank, sire?

THE KING.
>Yes, entirely frank.

DUKE DE BELLEGARDE (*boldly*).
  Well, then, I think him a great man!
THE KING.
  If needful
  You would proclaim it on the house-tops? Good!
  Can you not understand? The State, mark me,
  Is suffering, because he does it all
  And I am nothing!
DUKE DE BELLEGARDE.
  Ah!
THE KING.
  Rules he not war
  And peace, finances, states? Makes he not laws,
  Edicts, mandates, and ordinances too?
  Through treachery he broke the Catholic league;
  He strikes the house of Austria—friendly
  To me—to which the Queen belongs.
DUKE DE BELLEGARDE.
  Ah, sire,
  He lets you keep a vivary within
  The Louvre. You have your share.
THE KING.
  Then he intrigues With Denmark.
DUKE DE BELLEGARDE.
  But he let you fix the marc Among the jewelers.
THE KING (*whose ill-humor increases*).
  He fights with Rome!
DUKE DE BELLEGARDE.
  He let you issue an edict, alone,
  By which a citizen was not allowed

    To eat more than a crown's worth at a tavern,
    E'en though he wished to.
THE KING.
    All the treaties he Concludes in secret.
DUKE DE BELLEGARDE.
    Yes; but then you have
    Your hunting mansion at Planchette.
THE KING.
    All—all!
    He does it all! All with petitions rush
    To him! I'm but a shadow to the French!
    Is there a single one who comes to me
    For help?
DUKE DE BELLEGARDE.
    Those who have the king's evil come.
    [*The anger of* THE KING *increases.*
THE KING.
    He means to give my order to his brother!
    I will not have it! I rebel.
DUKE DE BELLEGARDE.
    But, sire—
THE KING.
    I am disgusted with his people!
DUKE DE BELLEGARDE.
    Sire!
THE KING.
    His niece, Combalet, leads a model life.
DUKE DE BELLEGARDE.
    'Tis slander, sire!

THE KING.
 Two hundred foot-guards!
DUKE DE BELLEGARDE.
 But Only a hundred horse-guards!
THE KING.
 What a shame!
DUKE DE BELLEGARDE.
 He saves France, sire.
THE KING.
 Does he? He damns my soul!
 With one arm fights the heathen, with the other
 He signs a compact with the Huguenots.
 [*Whispering to* DUKE DE BELLEGARDE.
 Then, if I dared to count upon my hand
 The heads—the heads that fall for him at Grève!
 All friends of mine! His purple robes are made
 Of their hearts' blood! 'Tis he who forces me
 To wear eternal mourning.
DUKE DE BELLEGARDE.
 Treats he his own More kindly? Did he spare Saint Preuil?
THE KING.
 He has A bitter tenderness, they say, for those He loves. He must love me tremendously!
 [*Abruptly, after a pause, folding his arms.*
 He has exiled my mother!
DUKE DE BELLEGARDE.
 But he thinks He does your will. He's faithful. He is firm
 And sure.
THE KING.
 I hate him! He is in my way.

He crushes me! I am not master here—
Not free! And yet I might be something. Ah,
When he walks o'er me with such heavy tread,
Does he not fear to rouse a slumbering king?
For trembling near me, be it ne'er so high,
His fortune vacillates with every breath
I draw, and all would crumble at a word,
Did I wish loud, what I wish in my heart!
[*A pause.*
That man makes good men bad, and bad men vile!
The kingdom, like the king, already sick,
Grows worse. Without is cardinal, within
Is cardinal; no king is anywhere!
He torments Austria, lets any one
Capture my vessels in Gascony's Bay.
Allies me with Gustavus Adolphus!
What more? I do not know. He's everywhere:
As if he were soul of the king, he fills
My kingdom, and my family, and me.
I am much to be pitied. [Going to window.
Always rain.

DUKE DE BELLEGARDE.
Your Majesty is suffering?
THE KING.
I am bored.
[*A pause.*
I am the first in France and yet the last!
I'd change my lot to lead a poacher's life—
To hunt all day; to have no cares to fret
The pleasures of the chase; to sleep 'neath trees;

To laugh at the King's officers, to sing
During the storm; to live as freely in the woods
As birds live in the air. The peasant in
His hut, at least, is master and is king;
But with that scarlet man forever there,
Forever stern and cold, and speaking thus,
"This must be your good pleasure, sire!" Oh, outrage!
This man conceals me from my people's gaze.
As with young children, he hides me beneath
His robe; and when a passer-by asks, "Who
Is that behind the Cardinal?" they say,
"The King!" Then there are new lists every day.
Last week the Huguenots; the duelists
To-day! He wants their heads. Such a great crime—
A duel! But the heads; what does he do
With them?
[DUKE DE BELLEGARDE *stamps his foot. Enter* MARQUIS DE NANGIS *and* MARION.

SCENE VII

The same. MARION, MARQUIS DE NANGIS. MARQUIS DE NANGIS *advances with his escort to within a few steps of* THE KING; *he kneels there.* MARION *falls on her knees at the door*

MARQUIS DE NANGIS.
  Justice, my sire.

THE KING.
    Against whom? Speak!
MARQUIS DE NANGIS.
    Against a cruel tyrant—against Armand,
    Called here the cardinal-minister!
MARION.
    Mercy, My sire!
THE KING.
    For whom?
MARION.
    For Didier!
MARQUIS DE NANGIS.
    And for him, Gaspard de Saverny!
THE KING.
    I've heard those names.
MARQUIS DE NANGIS.
    Justice and mercy, sire!
THE KING.
    What title?
MARQUIS DE NANGIS.
    Sire, I am uncle of one.
THE KING.
    And you?
MARION.
    I'm sister Unto the other!
THE KING.
    Why do you come here, Sister and uncle?
MARQUIS DE NANGIS (*indicating first one of* THE KING's *hands, then the other*).
    To entreat mercy

From this hand, and justice from that! My sire,
I, William, Marquis de Nangis, Captain
Of Hundred Lances, Baron of Mountain
And Field, do make appeal to my two lords—
The King of France and God, for justice 'gainst
Armand du Plessis, Cardinal Richelieu.
Gaspard de Saverny, for whom I make
This prayer, is my nephew—

MARION (*low to* MARQUIS DE NANGIS).
Oh, speak for both, My lord!

MARQUIS DE NANGIS (*continuing*).
Last month he had a duel with
A captain, a young nobleman, Didier.
Of parentage uncertain. 'Twas a fault.
They were too rash and brave. The minister
Had stationed sergeants—

THE KING.
Yes, I know the story. Well, what have you to say?

MARQUIS DE NANGIS.
That 'tis high time
You thought about these things! The Cardinal-Duke
Has more than one disastrous scheme afoot.
He drinks the best blood of your subjects, sire!
Your father, Henry IV., of royal heart,
Would not have sacrificed his nobles thus!
He never struck them down without dire need!
Well served by them, he sought to guard them well.
He knew good soldiers had more use in them
Than trunkless heads. He knew their worth in war,
This soldier-king whose doublet smelled of battle!

Great days were those. I shared, I honor them!
A few of the old race are living yet.
Never could priest have touched one of those lords.
There was no selling of a great head cheap!
Sire, in these treacherous days to which we've come,
Trust an old man, keep a few nobles by.
Perhaps, in your turn, you will need their help.
The time may come when you will groan to think
Of all the honors lavished on La Grève!
Then, sadly, your regretful eyes will seek
Those lords indomitably brave and true,
Who, dead so long, had still been young to-day.
The country's heart yet pants with civil war;
The tocsin of past years re-echoes yet,
Be saving of the executioner's arm!
He is the one should sheathe his sword, not we!
Be miserly with scaffolds, O my sire!
'Twill be a woful thing some later day
To mourn this great man's help, who hangs to-day
A whitening skeleton on gallows-tree!
For blood, my king, is no good, wholesome dew.
You'll reap no crops from irrigated Grève!
The people will avoid the sight of kings.
That flattering voice which tells you all is well,
Tells you you're son of Henry IV., and Bourbon—
That voice, my sire, however high it soars,
Can never drown the thud of falling heads!
Take my advice: play not this costly game.
You, King, are bound to look God in the face,
Hark to the words of fate, ere it rebels!

War is a nobler thing than massacre!
'Tis not a prosperous nor joyful State
When headsmen have more work than soldiers have!
He for our country is a pastor hard,
Who dares collect his tithes in slaughtered heads!
Look! this proud lord of inhumanity
Who holds your scepter has blood-covered hands!

THE KING.

The Cardinal's my friend! Who loves me must Love him!

MARQUIS DE NANGIS.

Sire!

THE KING.

Silence! He's my second self.

MARQUIS DE NANGIS.

Sire!

THE KING.

Bring no more such griefs to trouble me!
[*Showing his hair, which is beginning to turn gray.*
Petitioners like you make these gray hairs!

MARQUIS DE NANGIS.

An old man, sire; a woman, sire, who weeps! A word from you is life or death for us!

THE KING.

What do you ask?

MARQUIS DE NANGIS.

Pardon for my Gaspard!

MARION.

Pardon for Didier!

THE KING.

Pardons of a king Are often thefts from justice!

MARION.
>Oh, no, sire!
>Since God himself is merciful, you need
>Not fear! Have pity! Two young, thoughtless men,
>Pushed by this duel o'er a precipice
>To die! Good God! to die upon the gallows!
>You will have pity, won't you? I don't know
>How people talk to kings—I'm but a woman;
>To weep so much perhaps is wrong. But oh,
>A monster is that cardinal of yours.
>Why does he hate them? They did naught to him.
>He never saw my Didier. All who do
>Must love him! They're so young—these two! To die
>For just a duel! Think about their mothers.
>Oh, it is horrible! You will not do it, sire!
>We women cannot talk as well as men.
>We've only cries and tears and knees, which bend
>And totter as kings turn their eyes on us.
>They were in fault, of course! But if they broke
>Your law, you can forgive it! What is youth?
>Young people are so heedless! For a look,
>A word, a trifle, anything or nothing,
>They always lose their heads like that! Such things
>Are happening every day. Each noble, here,
>He knows it. Ask them, sire! Is it not true,
>My lords? Oh, frightful hour of agony!
>To know with one word you can save two lives!
>I'd love you all my life, sire, if you would
>Have mercy—mercy, God! If I knew how,
>I'd talk so that you'd have to say that word.

You'd pardon them; you'd say, "I must console
That woman, for her Didier is her soul."
I suffocate, sire. Pity, pity me!
THE KING.
Who is this woman?
MARION.
She's a sister, sire, Who trembles at your feet. You owe something Unto your people!
THE KING.
Yes! I owe myself To them, and dueling does grievous harm.
MARION.
You should have pity!
THE KING.
And obedience, too!
MARQUIS DE NANGIS.
Two boys of twenty years! Think of it well! Their years together are but half of mine!
MARION.
Your Majesty, you have a mother, wife, A son—some one at least who's dear to you! A brother? Then have pity for a sister!
THE KING.
No, I have not a brother! [*Reflects a moment.*
Yes, *Monsieur*!
[*Perceiving the escort of* MARQUIS DE NANGIS.
Well, my lord marquis, what is this brigade?
Are we besieged, or off to the Crusades?
To bring your guards thus boldly in my sight,
Are you a duke and peer?
MARQUIS DE NANGIS.
I'm better, sire, Than any duke and peer, created for mere

show! I'm Breton baron of four baronies.
DUKE DE BELLEGARDE (*aside*).
His pride is great, and here, unfortunate!
THE KING.
Good! To your manors carry back your rights, And leave us ours within our own domain. We are justiciary!
MARQUIS DE NANGIS (*shuddering*).
Sire, reflect! Think of their age, their expiated fault!
[*Falling on his knees.*
The pride of an old man, who, prostrate, kneels!
Have mercy!
[THE KING *makes an abrupt sign of anger and refusal.*
I was comrade to Henry!
Your father and our father! I was there
When he—that monster—struck the fatal blow.
'Til night I watched beside my royal dead:
It was my duty. I have seen my father
And my six brothers fall 'neath rival factions;
I have lost the wife who loved me. Now
The old man standing here is like a victim
Whom a hard executioner, for sport,
Has bound unto the wheel the whole long day.
My master, God has broken every limb
With His great iron rod! 'Tis night-time now,
And I've received the final blow! Farewell,
My king! God keep you!
[*He makes a profound obeisance, and exits.* MARION *lifts herself with difficulty, and, staggering, falls on the threshold of the gilt door of* THE KING's *private room.*
THE KING (*to* DUKE DE BELLEGARDE, *wiping his eyes and*

watching the retreating figure of MARQUIS DE NANGIS).
A sad interview!
Ah, not to weaken, kings must watch themselves!
To do right is not easy. I was touched.
[*Reflects for a moment, then interrupts himself suddenly.*
No pardoning to-day, for yesterday
I sinned too much!
[*Approaching* DUKE DE BELLEGARDE.
Before he came, my lord,
You said bold things, which may be bad for you
When I report to my lord cardinal
The conversation we have had. I'm sorry
For you, Duke. In the future, have more care!
I slept so wretchedly, my poor Bellegarde.
[With a gesture dismissing Courtiers and Guards.
Pray leave us, gentlemen!
[*To* L'ANGELY.] Stay, you!
[*All go out except* MARION, *whom* THE KING *does not see.*
DUKE DE BELLEGARDE *sees her crouching on the threshold of the door and goes to her.*

DUKE DE BELLEGARDE (*low to* MARION).
My child,
You can't remain here, crouching by this door;
What are you doing like a statue there?
Get up and go away!

MARION.
I'm waiting here For them to kill me!

L'ANGELY (*low to* DUKE DE BELLEGARDE).
Leave her there, my lord!
[*Low to* MARION.] Remain!

[*He returns to* THE KING, *who is seated in the great armchair and is in a profound reverie.*

SCENE VIII

THE KING, L'ANGELY

THE KING (*sighing deeply*).
  Ah! L'Angely, my heart is sick.
  'Tis full of bitterness. I cannot smile.
  You, only, have the power to cheer me. Come!
  You stand in no awe of my majesty.
  Come, throw a glint of pleasure in my soul.
  [*A pause.*
L'ANGELY.
  Life is a bitter thing, your Majesty.
THE KING.
  Alas!
L'ANGELY.
  Man is a breath ephemeral!
THE KING.
  A breath, and nothing more!
L'ANGELY.
  UnfortunateIs any one who is both man and king. Is it not true?
THE KING.
  A double burden—yes.

L'ANGELY.

And better far than life, sire, is the tomb, If but its gloom is deep enough!

THE KING.

I've thought That always!

L'ANGELY.

To be dead or unborn is The only happiness. Yes, man's condemned!

THE KING.

You give me pleasure when you talk like this!

[*A silence.*

L'ANGELY.

Once in the tomb, think you one e'er gets out?

THE KING (*whose sadness has increased with the Fool's words*).

We'll know that later. I wish I were there!

[*Silence.*

Fool, I'm unhappy! Do you comprehend?

L'ANGELY.

I see it in your face so thin and worn, And in your mourning—

THE KING.

Ah, why should I laugh?
Your tricks are lost on me! What use is life
To you? The fine profession! Jester to the King!
Bell out of tune, a jumping-jack to play with,
Whose half-cracked laugh is but a poor grimace!
What is there in the world for you, poor toy?
Why do you live?

L'ANGELY.

For curiosity.
But you—why should you live? I pity you!

I'd sooner be a woman than a king
Like you. I'm but a jumping-jack whose string
You hold; but underneath your royal coat
There's hid a tauter string, a strong arm holds.
Better a jumping-jack in a king's hands
Than in a priest's, my sire.
[*Silence.*]

THE KING (*thinking, growing more and more sad*).
You speak the truth,
Although you laugh. He is a fearful man!
Has Satan made himself a cardinal?
What if 'twere Satan who possessed my soul!
What say you?

L'ANGELY.
I have often had that thoughtMyself!

THE KING.
We must not speak thus. 'Tis a sin!
Behold, how dire misfortune follows me!
I had some Spanish cormorants. I come
To this place—not a drop of water here
For fishing! In the country! Not a pond
In this accursed Chambord large enough
To drown a flesh-worm! When I wish to hunt—
The sea! And when I wish to fish—the fields!
Am I unfortunate enough?

L'ANGELY.
Your lifeIs full of woe.

THE KING.
How will you comfort me?

L'ANGELY.
>   Another grief! You hold in high esteem,
>   And justly too, the art of training hawks
>   For hunting partridges. A good huntsman—
>   You're one—ought to respect the falconer.

THE KING.
>   The falconer! A god!

L'ANGELY.
>   Well! there are two Who are at point of death!

THE KING.
>   Two falconers?

L'ANGELY.
>   Yes!

THE KING.
>   Who are they?

L'ANGELY.
>   Two famous ones!

THE KING.
>   But who?

L'ANGELY.
>   Those two young men whose lives were begged of you!

THE KING.
>   Gaspard and Didier?

L'ANGELY.
>   Yes; they are the last.

THE KING.
>   What a calamity! Two falconers!
>   Now that the art is very nearly lost.
>   Unhappy duel! When I'm dead, this art
>   Will go from earth, as all things go at last!

Why did they fight this duel?
L'ANGELY.
   One declared That hawks upon the wing were not as swift
   As falcons.
THE KING.
   He was wrong. But yet that seems
   Scarcely a hanging matter— [*Silence.*
   And my right of pardon is inviolable—though
   I am too lenient, says the Cardinal! [*Silence.*
   [*To* L'ANGELY.] The Cardinal desires their death?
L'ANGELY.
   He does!
THE KING (*after pausing and reflecting*).
   Then they shall die!
L'ANGELY.
   They shall!
THE KING.
   Poor falconry!
L'ANGELY (*going to window*).
   Sire, look!
THE KING (*turns around suddenly*).
   At what?
L'ANGELY.
   Just look, I beg of you!
THE KING (*rising and going to the window*).
   What is it?
L'ANGELY (*indicating something outside*).
   They have changed the sentinel!
THE KING.
   Well, is that all?

L'ANGELY.
Who is that fellow with The yellow lace?
THE KING.
No one—the corporal!
L'ANGELY.
He puts a new man there. What says he, low?
THE KING.
The password! Fool! What are you driving at?
L'ANGELY.
At this: Kings act the part of sentinels.
Instead of pikes, a scepter they must bear.
When they have strutted 'round their little day,
Death comes—the corporal of kings—and puts
Another scepter-bearer in their place,
Speaking the password which God sends, and which
Is clemency.
THE KING.
No, it is justice. Ah,
Two falconers! It is a frightful loss!
Still, they must die.
L'ANGELY.
As you must die, and I.
Or big or little, death has appetite
For all. But though they've not much room,
The dead sleep well. The Cardinal annoys
And wearies you. Wait, sire! A day, a month,
A year; when we have played as long as needful—
I, my own part of fool; you, king; and he,
The master—we will go to sleep. No matter
How proud or great we are, no one shall have

More than six feet of territory there.

Look! how they bear his lordly litter now!

THE KING.

Yes, life is dark; the tomb alone is bright.

If you were not at hand to cheer me up—

L'ANGELY.

Alas! I came to-day to say farewell.

THE KING.

What's that?

L'ANGELY.

I leave you!

THE KING.

You're a crazy fool!

Death, only, frees from royal service.

L'ANGELY.

Well, I am about to die!

THE KING.

Have you gone mad?

L'ANGELY.

You have condemned me—you, the King of France!

THE KING.

If you are joking, fool, explain yourself.

L'ANGELY.

I shared the duel of those two young men—

At least my sword did, sire, if I did not.

I here surrender it.

[*Draws his sword and, kneeling, presents it to* THE KING.

THE KING (*takes it and examines it*).

Indeed, a sword! Where does it come from, friend?

L'ANGELY.
   We're noble, sire! The guilty are not pardoned. I am one.
THE KING (*somber and stern*).
   Good night, then! Let me kiss your neck, poor fool,
   Before they cut it off. [*Embraces* L'ANGELY.
L'ANGELY (*aside*).
   He's in dead earnest!
THE KING (*after a pause*).
   For never does a worthy king oppose
   The course of justice. But you claim too much,
   Lord Cardinal—two falconers and my fool!
   All for one duel!
   [*Greatly agitated, he walks up and down with his hand on his forehead. Then he turns to* L'ANGELY, *who is most anxious.*
   Go! console yourself!
   Life is but bitterness, the tomb means rest.
   Man is a breath ephemeral.
L'ANGELY (*aside*).
   The devil!
   [THE KING *continues to pace the floor and appears violently agitated.*
THE KING.
   And so, you think you'll have to hang, poor fool!
L'ANGELY (*aside*).
   He means it! God! I feel cold perspiration
   Starting upon my brow.
   [*Aloud.*] Unless a word From you—
THE KING.
   Whom shall I have to make me laugh?
   If you should rise from out the tomb, come back

And tell me all about it. 'Tis a chance!

L'ANGELY.

The errand is a pleasant one!

[THE KING *continues to walk rapidly, speaking to* L'ANGELY *now and then.*

THE KING.

What triumph For my lord cardinal—my fool!

[*Folding his arms.*

Think you I could be master if I wished to be?

L'ANGELY.

Montaigne would say, "Who knows?" And Rabelais, "Perhaps."

THE KING (*with gesture of determination*).

Give me a parchment, fool.

[L'ANGELY *eagerly hands a parchment which he finds on the table near the writing-desk.* THE KING *hastily writes a few words, then gives the parchment back to* L'ANGELY.

Behold! I pardon all.

L'ANGELY.

All three?

THE KING.

Yes.

L'ANGELY (*running to* MARION).

Come, madame, Come, kneel, and thank the King.

MARION (*falling on her knees*).

We have the pardon?

L'ANGELY.

Yes! It was I—

MARION.

Whose knees must I embrace—His Majesty's or yours?

THE KING (*astonished, examining* MARION: *aside*).

What does this mean? Is this a trap?

L'ANGELY (*giving parchment to* Marion).

Here is the pardon. Take it!

[MARION *kisses it, and puts it in her bosom.*

THE KING (*aside*).

Have I been duped?[*To* MARION.] One instant! Give it back!

MARION.

Good God!

[*To* THE KING, *with courage, touching her breast.*

Come here and take it, and tear out My heart as well!

[THE KING *stops and steps backward, much embarrassed.*

L'ANGELY (*low to* Marion).

Good! Keep it, and be firm! His Majesty won't take it, there!

THE KING (*to* Marion).

Give it To me!

MARION.

Take it, my sire!

THE KING (*casting down his eyes*).

Who is this siren?

L'ANGELY (*low to* Marion).

He wouldn't touch the corset of the Queen!

THE KING (*after a moment's hesitation, dismisses* MARION *with a gesture without looking at her*).

Well, go!

MARION (*bowing profoundly to* THE KING).

I'll fly to save the prisoners! [*Exits.*

L'ANGELY (*to* THE KING).

She's sister to Didier, the falconer.

THE KING.
>She can be what she will. It's very strange,
>The way she made me drop my eyes! Made me,
>A man— [*Silence.*
>Fool, you have played a trick on me!
>I'll have to pardon you a second time.

L'ANGELY.
>Yes, do it! Every time they grant a pardon, Kings lift a dreary weight from off their hearts.

THE KING.
>You speak the truth. I always suffer when
>La Grève holds court. Nangis was right: the dead
>Serve nobody. To fill Montfaucon
>I make a desert of the Louvre!
>[*Walking rapidly.*
>'Tis treason
>To strike my right of pardon out, before
>My face. What can I do? Disarmed, dethroned,
>And fallen: in this man absorbed, as in
>A sepulcher! His cloak becomes my shroud:
>My people mourn for me as for the dead.
>I am resolved: those two boys shall not die!
>The joy of living is a heavenly gift.
>[*After reflection.*
>God, who knows where we go, can ope the tomb;
>A king cannot. Back to their families
>I give them; that old man, that fair young girl,
>Will bless me. It is said: I've signed it—I,
>The King. The Cardinal will be furious,
>But it will please Bellegarde.

L'ANGELY.
One can, sometimes, Be kingly by mistake.

ACT V.

THE CARDINAL

SCENE.—*Beaugency. The tower of Beaugency. A courtyard; the tower in the background, all around a high wall. To the left, a tall arched door; to the right, a small rounded door in the wall; near the door a stone table and stone bench*

SCENE I

Some Workmen. They are pulling down a corner of the back wall on the left. The demolition is almost completed

FIRST WORKMAN (*working with his pickax*).
  It's very hard!
SECOND WORKMAN (*working*).
  Deuce take this heavy wall we're pulling down!
THIRD WORKMAN (*working*).
  Saw you the scaffold, Peter?
FIRST WORKMAN.
  Yes, I did.
  [*He goes to the large door and measures it.*

The door is narrow; never will the litter of the Lord Cardinal go through it.

THIRD WORKMAN.

Bah! Is it a house?

FIRST WORKMAN (*with affirmative gesture*).

With great long curtains. Yes. It takes some four and twenty men on foot to carry it.

SECOND WORKMAN.

I saw the great machine, One night when it was very dark. It looked Just like Leviathan in shadow-land.

THIRD WORKMAN.

What does he come here with his sergeants for?

FIRST WORKMAN.

To see the execution of those two young men. He's sick. He needs to be amused.

SECOND WORKMAN.

To work!

[*They resume work; the wall is about torn down.*

Saw you the scaffold, all in black? That comes of being noble!

FIRST WORKMAN.

They have everything.

SECOND WORKMAN.

I wonderIf they would build a black scaffold for us.

FIRST WORKMAN.

What have those young men done that they should die? Hein? Do you understand, Maurice?

THIRD WORKMAN.

I don't. It's justice.

[*They continue their work.* LAFFEMAS *enters;* THE WORKMEN *are silent. He comes from the back as though he were coming from an inside court of the prison; stops beside* THE WORKMEN, *appears to examine the breach, and gives them some directions. When the space is opened, he orders them to hang black cloth across it, which covers it entirely; then he dismisses them. At almost the same moment* Marion *appears, dressed in white, and veiled; she enters through the great door, crosses the court rapidly, and runs to the grating of the small door, at which she knocks.* LAFFEMAS *follows slowly in the same direction. The grating is opened;* THE TURNKEY *appears.*

SCENE II

MARION, LAFFEMAS

MARION (*showing a parchment to* THE TURNKEY).
Order of the King!
THE TURNKEY.
You can't Enter, madame.
MARION.
What!
LAFFEMAS (*presenting a paper to* THE TURNKEY).
Signed, the Cardinal!
THE TURNKEY.
Enter.
[*When about to enter,* LAFFEMAS *turns, looks at* MARION *a moment, then approaches her.* THE TURNKEY *shuts the door.*

LAFFEMAS (*to* MARION).
  You here? This questionable place!
MARION.
  I am. [*Triumphantly showing the parchment.*
  I have the pardon!
LAFFEMAS (*showing his*).
  Yes? I have the revocation!
MARION (*with a cry of horror*).
  Mine was yesterday—The morning!
LAFFEMAS.
  Mine, last night!
MARION (*with hands over her eyes*).
  My God! No hope!
LAFFEMAS.
  Hope is a flash of lightning which deceives.
  The clemency of kings is a frail thing;
  It comes with lagging steps and goes with wings.
MARION.
  The King was moved with pity for their fate!
LAFFEMAS.
  What can the King against the Cardinal?
MARION.
  Oh, Didier, our last hope's extinguished now!
LAFFEMAS (*low*).
  Not—not the last!
MARION.
  Just Heaven!
LAFFEMAS (*drawing near to her*).
  There is here a man whom one short word from you could make Happier than any king, and mightier too!

MARION.
 Away!
LAFFEMAS.
 Is that your answer?
MARION (*haughtily*).
 I beg you!
LAFFEMAS.
 How fleeting are the whims of the fair sex!
 You were not always, madame, so severe!
 Now that 'tis question of your lover's life—
MARION (*without looking at him, turning to the small door, her hands clasped*).
 If it would save your life, I could not go
 Back to that infamy. My soul's grown pure
 At touch of you, my Didier; sin is shamed.
 Your love gives back my lost virginity.
LAFFEMAS.
 Well, love him!
MARION.
 Ah, he pushes me from crime To vice! Oh, monster, go! Let me keep pure!
LAFFEMAS.
 There is but one thing left for me to do!
MARION.
 What is it?
LAFFEMAS.
 I can show you—let you see. It is to-night.
MARION (*trembling all over*).
 Oh, heaven! this night!

LAFFEMAS.

This night The Cardinal, in litter, will attend.

[MARION *is buried in a deep and painful reverie. Suddenly she passes her two hands over her brow and turns, as if wild, toward* LAFFEMAS.

MARION.

How could you manage their escape?

LAFFEMAS (*low*).

You mean? Two of my men could guard this place, by which The Cardinal passes—

[*He listens at the small door.*

I think some one comes!

MARION (*wringing her hands*).

You'll save him?

LAFFEMAS.

Yes.[*Low.*] To tell you in this place—The walls have echoes—elsewhere.

MARION (*with despair*).

Come!

[LAFFEMAS *goes toward the large door and signs to her to follow. She falls on her knees, turned toward the grating of the prison; then she arises with a convulsive effort and disappears through the great door after* LAFFEMAS. SAVERNY *and* DIDIER *enter, surrounded by Guards.*

SCENE III

DIDIER, SAVERNY. SAVERNY, *dressed in the latest fashion, enters gayly and petulantly.* DIDIER *is in black, walks slowly, is very pale. A jailer accompanied by Halberdiers conducts them.* THE JAILER *places the two Halberdiers as sentinels beside the black curtain.* DIDIER *sits, silently, on the stone bench*

SAVERNY (*to* THE JAILER, *who opens the door for him*).
 Thank you. The air is very good!
THE JAILER (*low, and drawing him aside*).
 My lord, two words with you.
SAVERNY.
 Four, if you like.
THE JAILER (*lowering his voice still more*).
 Will you escape?
SAVERNY (*eagerly*).
 Speak! How?
THE JAILER.
 That's my affair.
SAVERNY.
 Truly? [THE JAILER *nods his head.*
 Lord Cardinal,
 You meant to keep me from attending balls,
 But it appears I am to dance again.
 The pleasant thing that life is!
 [*To* THE JAILER.] When, my friend?
THE JAILER.
 To-night, as soon as it is dark.

SAVERNY.

   My faith! I shall be charmed to leave these quarters. Whence
   Comes this assistance?

THE JAILER.

   Marquis de Nangis.

SAVERNY.

   My good old uncle!
   [*To* THE JAILER.] 'Tis for both, I hope!

THE JAILER.

   I can save only one!

SAVERNY.

   For twice as much?

THE JAILER.

   I can save only one!

SAVERNY (*tossing his head*).

   Just one?
   [*Low to* The Jailer.] Then listen;
   Good jailer, that's the one to save!
   [*Indicating* DIDIER.

THE JAILER.

   You jest!

SAVERNY.

   I do not! He's the one!

THE JAILER.

   What an idea! Your uncle wants to save you, not save him.

SAVERNY.

   It's settled? Then prepare two shrouds at once.
   [*Turns his back on* THE JAILER, *who goes out, astonished. A*
   REGISTRAR *enters.*
   We can't be left alone an instant—strange!

REGISTRAR (*saluting the prisoners*).
   The royal councilor of the Great Chamber Is close at hand.
   [*Salutes them again and exits.*
SAVERNY.
   'Tis well! [*Laughing.* Annoying luck!
   Twenty years old—September—and to die Before October!
DIDIER (*motionless at front of stage, holding the portrait in his hand, and as if absorbed in a deep study of it*).
   Come, look at me well!
   Eyes in my eyes: thus. You are beautiful!
   What radiant grace! Hardly a woman, you!
   No: much more like an angel. God Himself
   When He formed that divinely honest look
   Put much fire in it but more chastity.
   That childish mouth, pushed open by sweet hopes,
   Throbs with its innocence.
   [*Throwing the portrait violently to the ground.*
   Why did that peasant
   Take me unto her breast? Why not have dashed
   My head against the stones? What did I do
   Unto my mother to be cursed with birth?
   Why, in that misery, it may be crime,
   Which forced her to abandon her own blood,
   Had she not motherhood enough to choke
   Me in her arms?
SAVERNY (*returning from back of court*).
   The swallows fly quite low;' Twill rain to-night.
DIDIER (*without hearing him*).
   A faithless, a mad thing,
   A woman is: inconstant, cruel, deep,

And turbulent as is the ocean. Ah,
Upon that sea I trusted all my fortune!
In all the vast horizon saw one star!
Well! I am shipwrecked! Nothing's left but death.
Yet I was born good-hearted: might have found
The spark divine within me by-and-by.
Fair looked the future! Oh, remorseless woman,
Did you not shrink in face of such a lie,
Since to your mercy I trusted my soul?

SAVERNY.

Forever Marion! You've strange ideas about her!

DIDIER (*without heeding him, picks up the picture and fixes his eyes upon it*).

Down 'mongst the degraded things
I must throw you, oh, woman who betrays!
A demon, with eyes touched by angels' wings.

[*Puts it back into his breast.*

Come back; here is your place!

[*Approaching* SAVERNY.] A curious thing!
That portrait is alive; I do not jest.
While you were sleeping there so peacefully
It gnawed my heart all night.

SAVERNY.

Alas! poor friend. We'll talk of death.

[*Aside.*] It comforts him, althoughI find it rather sad.

DIDIER.

What did you say?
I have not listened. Since I heard that name
I have been stupefied. I cannot think:
I can't remember, cannot hear nor see!

SAVERNY (*taking hold of his arm*).
   Death, friend!
DIDIER (*joyfully*).
   Oh, yes!
SAVERNY.
   Let's talk about it.
DIDIER.
   Yes!
SAVERNY.
   What is it, after all?
DIDIER.
   Did you sleep wellLast night?
SAVERNY.
   No, badly, for my bed was hard.
DIDIER.
   When you are dead, your bed will be much harder,
   But you will sleep extremely well—that's all.
   They've made hell splendidly; but by the side
   Of life, it's nothing.
SAVERNY.
   Good! My fears are gone!
   But to be hanged! That certainly is bad.
DIDIER.
   You're getting death; don't be an egotist.
SAVERNY.
   You can be satisfied; but I am not.
   I'm not afraid of death—that is no boast—
   When death is death, but on the gallows!
DIDIER.
   Well,

Death has a thousand forms—gallows are one.
That moment is not pleasant when the rope
Puts out your life as one puts out a flame,
Choking your throat to let your soul fly up;
But, after all, what matter? If all's dark,
If only all this earth is hidden well,
What matter if a tomb lies on one's breast?
What matter if the night-winds howl and blow
About the strings of flesh crows tore from you
When you were on the gibbet? What care you?
SAVERNY.
You're a philosopher.
DIDIER.
Yes, let them rave.
Let vultures tear my flesh, let worms consume,
As they consume all, even kings; my body
Is what's concerned, not I. What do I care?
When sepulchers shut down our mortal eye,
The soul lifts up the mighty mass of stone
And flies away—
[*A Councilor enters, preceded and followed by Halberdiers in black.*

SCENE IV

The same. COUNCILOR OF THE GREAT CHAMBER, *in full dress,* THE JAILER, *Guards*

THE JAILER (*announcing*).

    The Councilor of the King!

COUNCILOR (*saluting* SAVERNY *and* DIDIER *in turn*).

    My mission's painful and the law severe—

SAVERNY.

    I understand: there is no hope! Speak, sir!

COUNCILOR (*unfolds a parchment and reads*).

    "We, Louis, King of France and of Navarre,
    Reject appeals made by these men condemned,
    But moved by pity, change the punishment
    And order them beheaded."

SAVERNY (*joyfully*).

    God be praised!

COUNCILOR (*saluting them once more*).

    You are to hold yourselves in readiness;
    It will take place to-day.

[*He salutes and prepares to exit.*

DIDIER (*who has remained in the same thoughtful attitude, to* SAVERNY).

    As I was saying,
    After this death, although the corpse be mangled,
    Though every limb be stamped with hideous wounds,
    Though arms be twisted, broken every bone,
    Though through the mire the body has been dragged,
    From out that putrid, bleeding, awful flesh
    The soul shall rise, unstained, untouched, and pure.

COUNCILOR (*coming back, to* Didier).

    'Tis well to occupy yourselves with such Great thoughts.

DIDIER (*gently*).

    Please do not interrupt me, sir.

SAVERNY (*gayly to* Didier).
   No gallows!
DIDIER.
   Order of the fête is changed,
   I know. The Cardinal travels with his headsman,
   And he must be employed; the ax will rust.
SAVERNY.
   You're cool about it, yet the stake is great.
   [*To* THE COUNCILOR.] Thank you for such good news.
COUNCILOR.
   I wish 'twere better! Good sir, my zeal—
SAVERNY.
   Excuse me. What's the hour?
COUNCILOR.
   At nine o'clock to-night.
DIDIER.
   I hope the sky Will be as dark as is my soul.
SAVERNY.
   The place?
COUNCILOR (*indicating the neighboring court*).
   Here in the court. The Cardinal will come.
   [COUNCILOR *exits with his escort. The two prisoners remain alone. Day begins to fade. The halberds of the two sentinels, who silently promenade before the breach, are all that can be seen.*
DIDIER (*solemnly, after a pause*).
   At this portentous hour we must reflect
   Upon the fate awaiting us. Our years
   Are equal, though I'm older far than you.
   It is but just, therefore, that mine should be

The voice to cheer and to exhort you, since
I am the cause of all your misery.
'Twas I who challenged you. You were content
And happy: 'twas enough for me to pass
Across your life to ruin it. My fate
Pressed down upon yours 'til it crushed it. Now,
Together, we are soon to face the tomb.
We'll take each other's hand—
[*Sound of hammering.*
SAVERNY.
What is that noise?
DIDIER.
It is our scaffold which they're building, or Our coffins they are nailing.
[Saverny *sits on the stone bench.*
When the hour Has tolled, sometimes the heart of man gives way. Life holds us in a thousand secret ways.
[*A bell strikes.*
I think a voice is calling to us. Hark!
[*Another bell.*
SAVERNY.
The hour is striking.
[*A third bell.*
DIDIER.
Yes, the hour!
[*A fourth bell.*
SAVERNY.
In chapel!
[*Four more bells.*

DIDIER.
It is a voice that calls us, just the same.
SAVERNY.
Another hour!
[*He leans his elbows on the stone table and drops his head on his hands. The Guard is changed.*
DIDIER.
My friend, do not give way!
Don't falter on this threshold we must cross.
The tomb they're fitting up for us is low,
And won't permit the entrance of a head.
Let's go to meet them with a fearless tread.
The scaffold can afford to shake, not we.
They claim our heads; and since no fault is ours,
We'll bear them proudly to the fatal block.
[*Approaches Saverny, who is motionless.*
Courage!
[*Touches his arm and finds he is asleep.*
Asleep! While I've been preaching courage
This man has slept! What is my bravery
Compared to his? Sleep on, you who can sleep.
My turn will come—provided all things die,
That nothing of the heart survives within
The tomb, to hate what it has loved too much.
[*It is night. While* DIDIER *has become absorbed in his thoughts,* MARION *and* THE JAILER *enter through the opening in the wall;* THE JAILER *precedes her. He carries a dark-lantern and a bundle, both of which he places on the ground, then advances cautiously toward* MARION, *who has remained standing on the threshold, pale, motionless, half-wild.*

SCENE VI

[The scenes are mis-numbered in the book and skip from the number IV to the number VI in Act V. (note of etext transcriber)]

The same. MARION, THE JAILER

THE JAILER (*to* MARION.)
   Be sure to come at the appointed hour.
   [*Goes up stage; during the rest of this scene he continues to walk up and down at the back.*]
MARION (*advances with tottering steps as if absorbed in some desperate thought. Every now and then she draws her hand across her face as if to rub off something*).
   His lips, like red-hot iron, have branded me!
   [*Suddenly she discovers* DIDIER, *gives a cry, runs and throws herself breathless at his feet.*
   Didier—Didier!
DIDIER (*roused with a start*).
   Here, Marion! My God!
   [*Coldly.*] 'Tis you?
MARION.
   Who should it be? Oh, leave me here—
   Here at your feet! It is the place I love!
   Your hands, your dear loved hands, give them—your hands!
   Oh, they are wounded! Those harsh chains did that.
   The wretched creatures! But I'm here—you know—
   Oh, it is terrible! [*She weeps; her sobs are audible.*

DIDIER.

Why do you weep?

MARION.

Why? Didier, I'm not weeping! No, I laugh!

[*She laughs.*

We'll soon escape from here! I laugh. I'm happy.

You will live; the danger's passed.

[*She falls again at* DIDIER's *feet and sobs.*

My God! All this is killing me! I'm broken—crushed.

DIDIER.

Madame—

MARION (*rises, without hearing him, and gets the bundle and brings it to him*).

Now hurry! We have not much time!

Take this disguise. I've bribed the sentinels.

We'll leave Beaugency without being seen.

Go down that street, at the wall's end, out there!

The Cardinal will come to see them execute

His orders; we can't lose an instant now.

The cannon will be fired when he arrives,

And we'll be lost if we should still be here.

DIDIER.

'Tis well!

MARION.

Quick! hurry! Didier, you are saved!

To be free! Didier, how I love you—God!

DIDIER.

You say a street where the wall ends?

MARION.

I do.

I saw it. I've been there. It is quite safe.
I saw them close up the last window, too.
It may be we shall meet some women, but
They'll think you're just a passer-by. Come, love;
When you are far off—please put on these things—
We'll laugh to see you thus disguised. Come, dear!

DIDIER (*pushing the clothes aside with his foot*).

There is no hurry.

MARION.

Death waits at the door. Fly! Didier! Since I've come!

DIDIER.

Why did you come?

MARION.

To save you! What a question to ask me! Why such a freezing tone?

DIDIER (*with a sad smile*).

Ah, well! We menAre often senseless.

MARION.

We are losing time. The horses wait. What you have in your mind, You'll tell me afterward. We must fly now.

DIDIER.

Who is that man there watching us?

MARION.

The jailer. He's safe; I bribed him, as I did the guard.
Do you suspect them? You have such an air.

DIDIER.

It's nothing. We're so easily deceived.

MARION.

Come! Each lost moment chills me to the heart.
I seem to hear the tread of that great crowd.

Hasten, my Didier—on my knees—oh, fly!
DIDIER (*indicating* SAVERNY, *asleep*).
Tell me which one of us you want to save.
MARION (*overcome for a moment*).
[*Aside.*] Gaspard is generous: he would not tell.
[*Aloud.*] Does Didier speak to his beloved thus?
My Didier, what have you against me?
DIDIER.
Naught.
Lift up your face and look me in the eyes.
[MARION, *trembling, fixes her eyes on him.*
It is a perfect likeness! Yes.
MARION.
My love,
I worship you, but come!
DIDIER.
Don't turn away!
[*He looks at her fixedly.*
MARION (*terrified at his look*).
[*Aside.*] The kisses of that man, he sees them! God!
[*Aloud.*] You have a secret, something against me!
It hurts you! Tell me all about it, dear.
You know we often make things worse by thinking,
And too late find it out; then we regret.
I had my share in all your thoughts, love, once!
Speak, are those days for evermore gone by?
Do you not love me now? Have you forgot
My little room at Blois? Forgotten how
We loved each other, till the world was lost?
Sometimes you grew uneasy; then I said,

"If any one should see him!" Oh, 'twas fine!
But one day has destroyed it all. You've said
A thousand times, in words that burned my soul,
I was your love, I knew your secrets, I
Could make you anything I chose. What have
I ever asked? I've always thought with you!
This time, oh, yield to me! It is your life
I'm pleading for. My Didier, hark to me.
Alive or dead, I swear to follow you.
All things with you, love, will be sweet to me—
To fly, or die upon the scaffold. What!
You push me back? You shall not! Leave your hand,
I want it. My poor brow, it does no harm
To rest it on your knees. I am so tired;
I ran so fast to come! What would they say,
The people I knew once, to see me now?
I was so gay, so merry; now I weep!
What is it that you have against me? Speak!
Oh, shame! You must let me lie at your feet.
It's very cruel of you not to say
One single word. When we have thoughts, we speak!
'Twould be more merciful to stab me, love!
See, I have dried my tears, and I am smiling.
You smile too. Oh, if you don't smile at me,
I will not love you! I have always done
Just what you wanted; now it is your turn.
These chains are what have chilled your soul. Love, smile
And speak to me, and say "Marie."
DIDIER.
  "Marie" Or "Marion"?

MARION (*falls annihilated at his feet*).
    Didier, be merciful!
DIDIER (*with terrible tone*).
    Here, no one finds an entrance easily.
    Prisons of state are guarded night and day,
    The doors are iron, walls twenty cubits high;
    To open these remorseless doors, madame,
    To whom here did you prostitute yourself?
MARION.
    Who told you?
DIDIER.
    No one; but I understand.
MARION.
    Didier, I swear by every hope divine
    It was to save you, tear you from this place;
    To melt the executioner—to save you—
    Don't you hear?
DIDIER (*folding his arms*).
    I thank you! To descend
    As low as that! To have no shame, no soul!
    Oh, madame! can one be so infamous?
    [*Crossing the court with a great cry of rage.*
    Who is this trader in disgrace and vice,
    Who puts a price like that upon my head?
    Where is the jailer, where the judge, the man?—
    That I may crush him as I crush this thing.
    [*He is about to break the portrait in his hands, but he stops, and beside himself, continues.*
    The judge? Yes, gentlemen, make laws and judge!
    What matters it to me if the false weight

> Which swings your vile scales to this side or that
> Be made of woman's honor or man's life?
> [*To* MARION.] Go to your lover!

MARION.
> Do not treat me thus!
> Another word of scorn and I fall dead
> Here at your feet. If ever love was true
> And strong and pure, mine was. If any man
> Was ever worshiped by a woman, you
> Have been by me.

DIDIER.
> Hush! Do not speak! I might,
> For sorrow, have been born a woman too.
> I might have been as infamous as you.
> I might have sold myself, have given my breast
> To any passer-by, as place for rest.
> But if there came to me, in his frank way,
> An honest man, filled with the love of truth,
> If I had met a heart insane enough
> To keep its vain illusions all these years,
> Oh, sooner than not tell that honest man
> "I'm this," sooner than charm and dazzle him,
> Sooner than fail to warn him that my eyes
> So candid and my lips so pure were lies,
> Sooner than be perfidious and base like that,
> I'd want to dig my grave with my own hands.

MARION.
> O God!

DIDIER.
> How you would laugh if you could see

The picture that my heart painted of you!
How wise you were to shatter it, madame!
There you were chaste and beautiful and pure!
What injury has this poor man done you,
Who loved you on his bended knees?
[*Presenting portrait to her.*
Perhaps
This is a fitting time to give you back
This pledge of love ardent and true

MARION (*turning away with a cry*).

Oh, shame!

DIDIER.

Did you not have it painted just for me?
[*He laughs, and dashes the locket to the ground.*

MARION.

Will some one, out of pity, kill me now?

THE JAILER.

Time's passing.

MARION.

Yes, it flies; and we are lost.
Didier, I've not the right to say a single word.
I am a woman to whom naught is due.
You have rebuked and cursed me: you did well!
I merit still more hate and shame. You've been
Too kind; my broken, bruised heart is grateful.
But the remorseless hour draws near. Away!
The headsman you forget, remembers you.
I've planned it all. You can escape. Now, listen—
My God! do not refuse. You know how much
It costs me. Hate me, strike me, curse me, leave

Me to my shame, disown me, walk upon
My bleeding heart—but fly!
DIDIER.
Fly where? From whom?
There's naught but you to fly from in this world;
And I escape you, for the grave is deep.
THE JAILER.
The hour is passing.
MARION.
O my Didier, fly!
DIDIER.
I will not!
MARION.
Just for pity!
DIDIER.
Pity! why?
MARION.
To see you taken, bound! To see you—there!
Only to think it makes me die of horror!
Come! I will be a servant unto you.
Come! Take me, when I have redeemed myself,
Just to have something underneath your feet.
The one you called "a wife" in times of trial—
DIDIER.
A wife! [*Cannon sounds in the distance.*
This makes of you a widow, then!
MARION.
Didier!
THE JAILER.
The hour is past.

[*Rolling of drums. Enter* COUNCILOR OF THE GREAT CHAMBER, *accompanied by penitents bearing torches, and by* EXECUTIONER. *A crowd of soldiers and people follow.*
MARION.
 Ah, Christ!

SCENE VII

The same. COUNCILOR, EXECUTIONER, *Populace, Soldiers*

COUNCILOR.
 I'm ready, Gentlemen!
MARION (*to* DIDIER).
 I told you that he'd come!
DIDIER (*to* Councilor).
 We're ready also.
COUNCILOR.
 Which is named Gaspard, Marquis de Saverny?
[DIDIER *points to* SAVERNY, *who is asleep.*
 [*To* EXECUTIONER.] Awaken him!
EXECUTIONER (*shaking him*).
 How well he sleeps, my lord!
SAVERNY (*rubbing his eyes*).
 Ah, how could you Break in on such a pleasant sleep!
DIDIER.
 'Tis onlyInterrupted, friend!
SAVERNY (*half awake: sees* MARION *and salutes her*).
 Oh, I was dreaming

About you, my beauty!
COUNCILOR.
Have you made Your peace with God?
SAVERNY.
I have, sir.
COUNCILOR.
It is well. Please sign this paper!
SAVERNY (*takes the parchment, runs over it*).
'Tis the *procès-verbal*.
Good! This is a most curious thing—account
Of my own death, signed with my autograph!
[*Signs, and reads the paper again:* to COUNCILOR.
You have made three mistakes in spelling, sir.
[*Takes the pen and corrects them.* To EXECUTIONER.
You have awakened me; put me to sleep!
COUNCILOR (*to* DIDIER).
Didier!
[DIDIER *approaches:* COUNCILOR *gives pen to him.*
Your name is there.
MARION (*hiding her eyes*).
The grewsome thing!
DIDIER.
I could sign nothing with intenser joy!
[*The Guards form themselves into a line to lead them away.*
SAVERNY (*to some one in the crowd*).
Sir, step aside and let that young child see!
DIDIER (*to* Saverny).
My brother, 'tis for me you suffer death; Let us embrace each other! [*He embraces* SAVERNY.

MARION (*running to him*).
　And for me—No kisses, Didier!
DIDIER (*indicating* Saverny).
　This is my friend, madame!
MARION (*clasping her hands*).
　How hard you are upon me, a poor thing,
　Who always on my knees to king or judge
　Have begged mercy for you from every one!
　Pardon of them for you; pardon of you for me!
DIDIER (*rushes to Marion, trembling, and bursting into tears*).
　No, I cannot! The torture's horrible!
　No, I have loved too much to leave her so!
　It is too hard to keep a cold, impassive face
　When underneath the heart is breaking down.
　Come to my arms, oh, woman, come!
　[*Presses her convulsively to his heart.*
　I love you!
　I'm about to die. Before them all,
　It is my loftiest joy to tell you this:
　I love you!
MARION.
　Didier!
DIDIER.
　[*Embraces her again with rapture.*
　To my heart, oh, come!
　You who behold this direful tragedy,
　I wonder if there's one of you who would
　Refuse love unto one who'd given herself
　Entirely and unceasingly to him?
　Oh, I was wrong! Say, would you have me face

Eternity without a pardon from
Her lips? No! Stand by me and listen, love:
Among all womankind—and those who hear
Will prove me right by their own hearts—the one
I love, the one in whom I trust, the one
I venerate is you—is always you!
For you were kind, devoted, loving, good.
My life is almost ended. When death's near
A clearer light illuminates all things.
If you deceived me, 'twas excess of love;
And if you fell, have you not cruelly atoned?
Perhaps your mother—life's so hard—forgot
You in your cradle, as my mother did;
When you were young and helpless, perhaps they sold
Your innocence. Ah, lift up your white brow!
And listen, all of you. At such an hour
The earth is a mere shadow and the heart
Speaks true. Well, at this moment, from the height
Of the dread scaffold—and there's naught so high
When guiltless souls ascend it—here,
I say to you, Marie, angel of light,
Whose luster earth has dimmed, my love, my wife,
In God's name, before whom I soon shall stand,
I pardon you.

MARION (*suffocated with tears*).

Ah, Christ!

DIDIER.

It is your turn. Speak now, and pardon me!
[*He kneels before her.*

MARION.
　Didier!
DIDIER.
　Your pardon,
　Love! I was the most at fault, the most
　Unkind. God has chastised you much through me.
　Weep for me when I'm gone, because to have
　Hurt you is such a burden to take hence
　Into eternity. Don't leave it on me;
　Pardon me!
MARION (*inaudibly*).
　Have mercy on me—God!
DIDIER.
　Just speak one word; put your sweet hands upon
　My forehead. If your heart is full and you
　Can't speak, please make a sign. I'm dying; you
　Must comfort me.
　[MARION *places her hand on his forehead; he rises, embraces her tenderly, with a smile of celestial joy.*
　Farewell! Come, gentlemen!Let us move on!
MARION (*throws herself wildly between him and the Soldiers*).
　Oh, no! Stop! This is madness!
　If you think you can behead him easily,
　You have forgotten I am here. Spare us!
　Oh, men! oh, soldiers, judge, people! Spare us!
　How do you want me to ask you? Upon
　My knees? Well, here I am! Now if
　In you there's anything that quivers at
　A woman's voice, if God has thrown no curse
　On you—don't kill him!

[*To the spectators.*] Men and women—you!
When you go back into your homes to-night,
You'll find your mothers and your daughters; they
Will say to you, "It was a wicked crime.
You might have saved him, and you did not. Shame!"
Didier, they ought to know that I must follow
You! They will not kill you if they want
To keep me living!

DIDIER.

Let me die, Marie.
'Tis better, dear one, for my wound is deep;
It would have taken too much time to heal.
Better for me to go; but if, some time—
You see I'm weeping too—another comes,
A happier man, more fortunate than I,
Think of your old friend sleeping in the tomb.

MARION.

You shall not die! Are these men all inhuman?
You must live!

DIDIER.

Don't ask things impossible.
No; with your bright eyes, turn, illuminate
My grave for me. Embrace me. You will love
Me better, dead. I'll hold a sacred place
In your dear memory. But if I lived,
Lived near you with my lacerated soul—
I, who have loved no one but you—you see
It would be painful. I would make you weep.
I'd have a thousand thoughts I could not speak.
I'd seem to doubt you, watch you, worry you.

You would be most unhappy. Let me die!
COUNCILOR (*to* Marion).
The Cardinal will pass by soon, madame!
You can ask pardon for him then.
MARION.
Oh, yes!
The Cardinal is coming—that is true.
You'll see, then, gentlemen, that he will hear!
My Didier, you shall hear me talk to him!
The Cardinal! Indeed, you must be all insane,
To think such an old man—a Christian too,
The gracious Cardinal—will not be glad
To pardon you. Have you not pardoned me?
[*Nine o'clock strikes.* DIDIER *makes sign to all to hush.* MARION *listens with terror. After the nine strokes have sounded,* DIDIER *goes and stands close to* Saverny.
DIDIER (*to the spectators*).
You who have come to see the last of us,
If any speak of us, bear witness all,
That without faltering we have heard the hour
Bring us its summons to eternity.
[*The cannon sounds at the door of the tower; the black veil which concealed the opening in the wall, falls: the gigantic litter of* THE CARDINAL *appears, borne by twenty-four foot-guards, surrounded by twenty other guards bearing halberds and torches: the litter is scarlet and ornamented with the arms of the House of Richelieu. It crosses the back of the stage slowly. Great agitation among the crowd.*
MARION (*dragging herself up to the litter on her knees and*

wringing her hands).

In your Christ's name! In name of all your race, Mercy for them, my lord!

A VOICE (*from the litter*).

No mercy!

[MARION *falls to the ground. The litter passes and the procession of the condemned men follows it. The crowd rush madly after them.*

MARION (*alone, lifts herself half way up, and drags herself along by her hands: looking around.*)

Ah!

What did he say? Where are they gone? My love!

My Didier! No one! Not a sound! Is it

A dream—this place? the crowd?—or am I mad?

[*The people rush back in disorder. The litter reappears in the background on the side where it went off. Marion rises and gives a terrible cry.*

He's coming back!

GUARDS (*pushing the people aside*).

Make way!

MARION (*erect and half-wild, pointing to the litter*).

Look, all of you!

It is the red man who goes by!

[*She falls senseless.*

ESMERALDA

DRAMATIS PERSONÆ

- Esmeralda.
- Phœbus de Chateaupers.
- Claude Frollo.
- Quasimodo.
- Fleur-de-lys.
- Madame Aloise de Gondelaurier.
- Diana.
- Bérangère.
- Viscount de Gif.
- M. de Chevreuse.
- M. de Morlaix.
- Clopin Frouillefou.
- The Town-Crier.

Populace, Vagrants, Archers, etc.

ESMERALDA

ACT I

SCENE.—*The Court of Miracles. It is night. A crowd of vagrants. Noisy dancing. Male and female beggars in different attitudes of their profession. The King of Thune on his cask. Fires, lights, torches. In the shadow a circle of wretched dwellings*

SCENE I

CLAUDE FROLLO, CLOPIN FROUILLEFOU, *then* ESMERALDA, *then* QUASIMODO. THE VAGRANTS

CHORUS OF VAGRANTS.
 Long live Clopin! Long live the King of Thune!
 Long live the rogues of Paris.
 Let us strike our blows at dusk—
 The hour when all the cats are drunk.
 Let us dance! Defy Pope and bull,
 And let us laugh in our skins,

Whether April wets or June burns
The feathers in our caps.
Let us smell from afar
The shot of the avenging archer,
Or the bag of money which passes
On the back of the traveler.
In the light of the moon,
We will go dance with the spirits.
Long live Clopin, King of Thune!
Long live the rogues of Paris!

CLAUDE FROLLO (*apart behind a pillar in a corner of the stage. He is covered with a long cloak which hides his priestly garb*).

In the midst of this infamous band
What matters the sigh of a soul?
I suffer! Oh, never did fiercer flame
Burn in the bowels of a volcano.

[ESMERALDA *enters, dancing.*

CHORUS.

There she is! There she is! It is she—Esmeralda!

CLAUDE FROLLO (*aside*).

It is she! oh, yes—'tis she!
Wherefore, relentless fate,
Made you her so beautiful,
Me—so unfortunate?

[*She reaches the center of the stage. The Vagrants form an admiring circle around her.*

ESMERALDA.

An orphan am I,
Child of woe,

To you I turn
And flowers throw!
In my wild joy
Sad sighs abide;
I show a smile,
The tears I hide.

Poor girl—I dance
Where brooklets run,
As chirp the birds
My song flows on:
I am the dove
Which, hurt, must fall;
Over my cradle
Hangs death's pall.

CHORUS.
Young girl, dance on!
More gentle you make us.
Take us for family,
And play with us,
As stoops the nightingale
Unto the sea,
Teasing its waves
To ecstasy.

'Tis the young girl—
Child of woe,
When beams her eye
Grief must go.
She's like the bee

Which trembling flies
To the flower's heart,
Its Paradise.

Young girl, dance on!
More gentle you make us.
Take us for family,
And play with us!

CLAUDE FROLLO (*aside*).
Tremble, young girl—
The priest is jealous.

[CLAUDE *attempts to draw near to* ESMERALDA; *she turns away from him with a kind of horror. The procession of the Pope of Fools enters. Torches, lanterns and music. In the middle of the procession, upon a litter surrounded with candles,* QUASIMODO, *decked with cope and miter, is carried.*

CHORUS.
Salute him, clerks of Vasoche!
Shell-heaps, lubbers, beggars!
Salute him, all of you! He comes.
Behold the Pope of Fools!

CLAUDE FROLLO (*perceiving* Quasimodo, *and starting toward him with a gesture of anger*).
Quasimodo! What a strange part to play!
Profanation! Here—Quasimodo!

QUASIMODO.
Great God! what do I hear?

CLAUDE FROLLO.
Come here, I tell you.

QUASIMODO (*jumping from the litter*).

Here I am!

CLAUDE FROLLO.

Be anathematized!

QUASIMODO.

God! it is himself!

CLAUDE FROLLO.

Outrageous audacity!

QUASIMODO.

Moment of terror.

CLAUDE FROLLO.

To your knees, traitor!

QUASIMODO.

Pardon me, Master!

CLAUDE FROLLO.

No! I am a priest.

[CLAUDE FROLLO *tears off* QUASIMODO'S *pontifical ornaments, and crushes them underfoot.* THE VAGRANTS *begin to murmur; they form menacing groups around him; he looks at them angrily.*

THE VAGRANTS.

He threatens us,

O comrades!

Here in this place,

Where we reign.

QUASIMODO.

What means the audacity

Of these robbers?

They menace him,

But we shall see!

CLAUDE FROLLO.
> Race unclean,
> You menace me.
> Robbers—Jews—
> But we shall see!
> [*The anger of* THE VAGRANTS *bursts forth.*

THE VAGRANTS.
> Stop! stop! stop!
> Down with the mar-joy!
> He shall pay for it with his head;
> In vain he defends himself.

QUASIMODO.
> Have respect for his head.
> Let every one cease,
> Or I change this festival
> To a bloody battle.

CLAUDE FROLLO.
> It is not about his head
> That Frollo is troubled.
> [*Puts his hand on his heart.*
> There is the tempest,
> There is the battle!
> [*At the moment when* THE VAGRANTS' *fury has reached its highest pitch,* CLOPIN FROUILLEFOU *appears at the back of the stage.*

CLOPIN.
> Who in this infamous den
> Dares to attack my lord the Archdeacon,
> And Quasimodo, bell-ringer
> Of Notre Dame?

THE VAGRANTS (*subsiding*).

It is Clopin, our King!

CLOPIN.

Clowns! Be off!

THE VAGRANTS.

We must obey!

CLOPIN.

Leave us!

[THE VAGRANTS *retire to their hovels. The Court of Miracles appears deserted.* CLOPIN *approaches* CLAUDE *cautiously.*

SCENE II

CLAUDE FROLLO, QUASIMODO, CLOPIN FROUILLEFOU

CLOPIN.

What purpose brings you to this orgy?

Has your lordship any orders to give me?

You are my master in sorcery;

Speak—I will do all.

CLAUDE FROLLO (*grasping* CLOPIN'S *arm excitedly, and dragging him to the front of the stage*).

I have come to end all.

Listen!

CLOPIN.

My lord!

CLAUDE FROLLO.

I love her more than ever.

You behold me quivering with love and with anguish.
I must have her to-night.

CLOPIN.
You will see her pass by here—in a moment;
It is the way to her home.

CLAUDE FROLLO (*aside*).
Oh! Hell has hold of me!
[*Aloud.*] Soon—you say?

CLOPIN.
Upon the instant!

CLAUDE FROLLO.
Alone?

CLOPIN.
Alone.

CLAUDE FROLLO.
That is enough.

CLOPIN.
Will you wait?

CLAUDE FROLLO.
I wait—Let me have her, or let me die!

CLOPIN.
Can I help you?

CLAUDE FROLLO.
No!

[*He motions to* CLOPIN *to leave him, after having thrown him his purse. When he finds himself alone with* QUASIMODO, *he draws him to the front of the stage.*

CLAUDE FROLLO.
Come! I need you!

QUASIMODO.

It is well!

CLAUDE FROLLO.

For a deed that is impious, frightful, awful!

QUASIMODO.

You are my lord and master!

CLAUDE FROLLO.

Chains, death, the law—We brave them all.

QUASIMODO.

Count upon me.

CLAUDE FROLLO (*recklessly*).

I mean to abduct the gypsy!

QUASIMODO.

Master, take my blood—without telling me why!

[*Upon a sign from* Claude Frollo *he retires up stage and leaves his master down stage.*

CLAUDE FROLLO.

Oh, Heaven! to have given one's mind to the depths,
To have tried all the crimes of sorcery,
To have fallen lower than hell itself:
A priest, at midnight, in the dark to watch for a woman!
And to reflect that in this state in which I find my soul God sees me!

Well! what does it matter?
Fate drags me on!
Its hand is too strong,
Its will be done!
I begin life over—
The priest insane

Feels hope no longer,
Knows terror is vain!
Demon, who drugs me,
Give her to me;
And I, who evoked thee,
Thy slave will be—
Receive the priest
Whose bonds are riven!
Hell with her
Will be my heaven!
Come, exquisite woman,
Your beauty I claim.
You shall own me forever—
I swear, in God's name!
Since he—since the master
By whom love was given,
Bids me choose—me, a priest,
Between passion and heaven!

QUASIMODO (*returning*).
Master, the moment is at hand!

CLAUDE FROLLO.
Yes—the solemn hour:It will decide my fate. Be silent! Hush!

CLAUDE FROLLO *and* QUASIMODO.
The night is dark,
Footsteps I hear:
In shadow does not
Some one draw near?

[*They go to the back of the stage to listen.*

THE WATCH (*passing behind the houses*).
Vigilance and peace!

Whoever passes here
Must ope the eye to darkness,
To silence strain the ear.

CLAUDE FROLLO *and* QUASIMODO.
In shadow they come;
They make no sound:
Still let us be
While the watch goes round!

[*The voices of the watch grow fainter.*]

QUASIMODO.
The watch has passed!

CLAUDE FROLLO.
Our terror follows it.

[CLAUDE FROLLO *and* QUASIMODO *look anxiously at the door through which* ESMERALDA *must pass.*

QUASIMODO.
Love inspires,
Hope renders strong,
Him who watches
While sleeps the throng.
I see her come—
Lo! she appears.
Maid divine!
Have no fears!

CLAUDE FROLLO.
Love inspires,
Hope renders strong,
Him who watches
While sleeps the throng.
I see her come,

Maid divine!
Lo! she appears—
She is mine!
[ESMERALDA *enters: they throw themselves upon her and try to drag her away: she struggles.*
ESMERALDA.
Help—help! To me—help!
CLAUDE FROLLO *and* QUASIMODO.
Hush, young maiden—hush!

SCENE III

ESMERALDA, QUASIMODO, PHŒBUS DE CHATEAUPERS, *the archers of the watch*

PHŒBUS (*entering at the head of a body of archers*).
In the King's name!
[*In the struggle* CLAUDE *escapes. The archers seize* QUASIMODO.
PHŒBUS.
Arrest him! hold him close!
Be he lord or valet!
At once—we will conduct him
To the prison Chatelet.
[*The archers take* QUASIMODO *up stage and off.* ESMERALDA, *recovered from her fright, approaches* PHŒBUS *with curiosity, mingled with admiration, and draws him gently to the front of the stage.*

ESMERALDA (*to* PHŒBUS).
   Deign to tell me
   Your name, sir!
   I beg you to.
PHŒBUS.
   Phœbus, my child—
   Of the family
   Of Chateaupers.
ESMERALDA.
   Captain?
PHŒBUS.
   Yes, my queen!
ESMERALDA.
   Queen? oh, no!
PHŒBUS.
   Exquisite grace!
ESMERALDA.
   Phœbus! I like your name!
PHŒBUS.
   Upon my soul
   I have a blade
   Which has, Madame,
   Great havoc made.
ESMERALDA (*to* Phœbus).
   A beautiful captain,
   An officer grand,
   With corselet of steel
   And an air of command!
   Often, kind sir,
   Our hearts they break,

  And only laugh
  At the tears they make.
PHŒBUS (*aside*).
  With a beautiful captain,
  An officer gay,
  Love hardly succeeds
  In living a day.
  All soldiers desire
  To pluck every rose,
  Joys without troubles,
  Love without woes.
PHŒBUS (*to* Esmeralda).
  A radiant spirit
  Smiles at me
  Through thine eyes.
ESMERALDA.
  A beautiful captain,
  An officer grand,
  With corselet of steel
  And an air of command!
  Long watches the girl
  He carelessly passed;
  And the dreams he awakened
  Forever may last!
PHŒBUS.
  With a beautiful captain,
  An officer gay,
  Love hardly succeeds
  In a living day!
  It's like lightning which flashes—

This eager desire
Which the eyes of sweet maidens
Kindle to fire!

ESMERALDA (*standing before the* Captain *and admiring him*).
My lord Phœbus! Let me see you!
Let me admire you a hundred-fold!
Oh the beautiful scarf of silk—
Oh the fine scarf with fringe of gold!
[PHŒBUS *takes it off and offers it to her.*

PHŒBUS.
Does it please you?

ESMERALDA (*taking the scarf and putting it on*).
Yes, it is beautiful!

PHŒBUS.
One moment!
[*He goes to her and tries to embrace her.*

ESMERALDA (*drawing back*).
Don't, I beg you!

PHŒBUS (*insisting*).
You must kiss me!

ESMERALDA (*drawing away still more*).
No, truly!

PHŒBUS (*laughing*).
A beauty
So cruel,
So haughty,
Is charming.

ESMERALDA.
No, beautiful captain,
In vain you plead!

Can I tell how far
A kiss might lead?
PHŒBUS.
I am a captain,
Why abuse me?
I want a kiss—
Don't refuse me!
Give it me—give it, or I will take!
ESMERALDA.
No, leave me! I beg of you, for my sake.
PHŒBUS.
One kiss, one kiss—'tis nothing, you see.
ESMERALDA.
Nothing to you, but much to me!
PHŒBUS.
Look at me, dear! I am playing no part!
ESMERALDA.
Alas, but I cannot look into my heart!
PHŒBUS.
To-night love shall make an entrance there!
ESMERALDA.
Wherever love enters, soon follows despair.
[*She slips out of his arms and escapes.* PHŒBUS, *disappointed, turns to* QUASIMODO, *whom the archers hold bound at the back of the stage.*
PHŒBUS.
She escapes me, she resists me!
A gay adventure, verily!
I keep the worst of our two birds of prey—
The owl remains; the nightingale flew away!

[*He places himself at the head of his guard and goes out, taking* QUASIMODO *with him.*
CHORUS OF THE WATCH.
    Vigilance and peace—
    Whoever passes here
    Must ope the eye to darkness,
    To silence strain the ear!
[*The sound grows fainter and finally ceases.*

ACT II

SCENE.—*The square of Grève. The pillory.* Quasimodo *is in the pillory. Populace on the square*

SCENE I

CHORUS.
    He abducted a girl—
    What! is it possible?
    Hark! how they abuse him!
    Do you hear, my friends?
    Quasimodo has been hunting on Cupid's domain!
A WOMAN OF THE PEOPLE.
    He will pass through my street
    On his return from the pillory;
    And it is Pierrat Forterne
    Who will give us the signal.

TOWN-CRIER.
　In the King's name, whom God protect!
　The man you see here, will be put
　Under a strong guard,
　In the pillory for one hour.
CHORUS.
　Down with him! Down with him!
　The hunchback, the deaf, the one-eyed creature
　This Barabbas!
　I believe, s'death! he's looking at us.
　Down with the sorcerer!
　He makes faces, he kicks;
　He makes dogs bark in the streets.
　Punish the rascal well!
　Double the whip and the penalty.
QUASIMODO.
　Drink!
CHORUS.
　Hang him!
QUASIMODO.
　Drink!
CHORUS.
　Be accursed!
　[ESMERALDA, *some instants ago, joined the crowd. She perceives* QUASIMODO, *first with surprise, then with pity. Suddenly, in the midst of all the noise, she mounts the pillory, unfastens a little cup which she carries on her belt, and gives a drink to* QUASIMODO.
CHORUS.
　What are you doing, beautiful girl?

Leave Quasimodo alone!
When Beelzebub roasts,
Nobody gives him water.
[*She comes down. The archers unfasten* Quasimodo *and take him away.*
CHORUS.
He abducted a woman!
Who? This dolt!
It is terrible, it is infamous,
It is too much!
Do you hear, my friends?
Quasimodo
Dared to go hunting on Cupid's domain.

SCENE II

A magnificent drawing-room in which people are making preparations for a festival. PHŒBUS, FLEUR-DE-LYS, MADAME ALOISE DE GONDELAURIER

MADAME ALOISE.
Phœbus, my future son-in-law, listen to me. I am fond of you.
Be master here, as if you were another self.
Look to it that every one is gay to-night.
And you, my daughter, come, get ready.
You will be the most beautiful at this festival,
Be also the most happy.
[*She goes up stage and gives orders to the servants, who*

continue the preparations.
FLEUR-DE-LYS.
   Sir, since the other week,
   We have hardly seen you twice!
   This festival brings you back.
   How fortunate for us!
PHŒBUS.
   Don't scold, I beg of you!
FLEUR-DE-LYS.
   I understand. Phœbus forgets me!
PHŒBUS.
   I swear to you—
FLEUR-DE-LYS.
   Don't swear! They only swear who deceive.
PHŒBUS.
   Forget you? What folly!
   Are you not the most fair?
   Am I not the most loving?
PHŒBUS (*aside*).
   My beautiful betrothed
   Is out of sorts to-day;
   Suspicion is in her mind.
   What a pity!
   Beauties, the lovers you treat ill
   Go elsewhere.
   You can do more with pleasure
   Than with tears.
FLEUR-DE-LYS (*aside*).
   To betray me, his betrothed,
   Who belong to him!

I, who have only him to think of
And worry about!
Ah! whether he is away or here,
What grief!
Present, he scorns my joy;
Absent, my tears.

FLEUR-DE-LYS.
Phœbus, the scarf that I worked for you—
What have you done with it? I don't see it.

PHŒBUS (*troubled*).
The scarf? I don't know!
[*Aside.*] Good God! unlucky chance!

FLEUR-DE-LYS.
You forgot it?
[*Aside.*]To whom has he given it?
And for whom am I deserted?

MADAME ALOISE (*coming up to them and trying to reconcile them*).
Heavens! get married! Then you can quarrel.

PHŒBUS (*to* FLEUR-DE-LYS).
No! I have not forgotten it.
I remember, I carefully folded it
And put it in an enameled box
That I had made for it.
[*Passionately to* FLEUR-DE-LYS, *who still frets.*
I swear I love you better
Than one could love Venus herself!

FLEUR-DE-LYS.
Don't swear! Don't swear!
They only swear who deceive!

MADAME ALOISE.
　Children, don't quarrel—everything is bright to-day!
　Come, my daughter, you must be seen!
　The guests are coming! Everything has its turn.
　[*To the servants.*] Light the candles and let the ball begin.
　I want everything to be beautiful, to seem as bright as day.
PHŒBUS.
　Since we have Fleur-de-lys, nothing is wanting to the ball.
FLEUR-DE-LYS.
　Yes, Phœbus—love is wanting! [*They go out.*
PHŒBUS (*watching* Fleur-de-lys *go out*).
　She speaks the truth: my heart is sad
　Even when she is near—
　The one I love, the one who fills my soul—
　Alas! she is not here.

　Exquisite creature,
　To you my love!
　Oh, dancing shadow,
　My sweet-voiced dove,
　Absent, yet with me
　Wherever I move!

　She's as bewildering and sweet
　As is a nest 'mid rushes,
　Sweet as a rosebud crowned with moss,
　Sweet as the joy which sorrow hushes.

　Humble child and virgin proud,
　Soul that's pure though free!

Voluptuous ardors sink abashed
Before thy chastity.

In the dark night she comes,
An angel from the skies;
Her forehead veiled by shadows,
Flames darting from her eyes.

I see her face forever—
Now bright, now dark it seems;
But strangely—'tis in heaven
I see her in these dreams.

Exquisite creature.
To you my love!
Oh, dancing shadow,
My sweet-voiced dove,
Absent, yet with me
Wherever I move!

[*Enter several lords and ladies in gala dress.*]

SCENE III

The preceding. VISCOUNT DE GIF, M. DE MORLAIX, M. DE CHEVREUSE, MADAME DE GONDELAURIER, FLEUR-DE-LYS, DIANA, BÉRANGÈRE. *Ladies, Lords*

VISCOUNT DE GIF.
    My salutations, noble hostesses!
MADAME ALOISE, PHŒBUS, FLEUR-DE-LYS (*bowing*).
    Good-evening, noble viscount!
    Forget all care and grief
    Beneath this hospitable roof.
M. DE MORLAIX.
    Ladies, may God send you
    Health, pleasure, and happiness!
MADAME ALOISE, PHŒBUS, FLEUR-DE-LYS.
    May Heaven return with interest
    All your good wishes, my lord!
M. DE CHEVREUSE.
    Ladies, from the bottom of my soul
    I belong to you, as I do to God!
MADAME ALOISE, PHŒBUS, FLEUR-DE-LYS.
    Kind sir, may our good Lady
    Come always to your aid!
    [*All the guests enter.*
CHORUS.
    Come to the festival, come!
    Page, lordship, and ladyship, come!
    With flowers in your hand,
    A joy-seeking band,
    Come to the festival, come!
    [*The guests greet and salute each other; servants circulate among the crowd, bearing platters laden with flowers and fruits. A group of young girls forms itself near a window to the left. Suddenly one of them calls to the others, and motions to them to look out of the window.*

DIANA (*looking out*).

　Come and look! come and look, Bérangère!

BÉRANGÈRE (*looking into the street*).

　Isn't she quick? Isn't she light?

DIANA.

　It is a fairy or it is love.

VISCOUNT DE GIF (*laughing*).

　Who dances in the public square?

M. DE CHEVREUSE (*after having looked*).

　Indeed! it is the magician.

　Phœbus, it is your gypsy

　Whom, the other night, with valor

　You saved from a robber.

VISCOUNT DE GIF.

　Oh, yes, it is the gypsy.

M. DE MORLAIX.

　She's as beautiful as the day.

DIANA (*to* Phœbus).

　If you know her, tell her to come

　And dance for us.

PHŒBUS (*looking out with an absent air*).

　It might be she!

　[*To* M. DE GIF.] Do you think she would remember?

FLEUR-DE-LYS (*who watches and listens*).

　Every one remembers you.

　Come, call her, tell her to come up.

　[*Aside.*] I will see whether to believe what I am told.

PHŒBUS (*to* Fleur-de-lys).

　You wish it? Well, let us try!

　[*He motions to the dancer to come up.*

THE YOUNG GIRLS.
  She is coming!
M. DE CHEVREUSE.
  She has disappeared under the porch.
DIANA.
  She has left the mob, stupefied.
VISCOUNT DE GIF.
  Ladies, you will see the nymph of the streets.
FLEUR-DE-LYS (*aside*).
  How quickly she obeyed that sign from Phœbus!

SCENE IV

The same. ESMERALDA. *The gypsy enters timidly, confused and radiant. Movement of admiration. The crowd falls back before her*

CHORUS.
  Look! her brow is fair amid the fairest,
  As a star would shine, surrounded by torches.
PHŒBUS.
  Oh, creature divine!
  Admiration is duty.
  Of this ball she is queen,
  Her crown is her beauty.
  [*He turns to* MESSIEURS DE GIF *and* DE CHEVREUSE.

  Friends, my soul is on fire.

War and death would I face,
To hold in my arms
Such bewildering grace.

M. DE CHEVREUSE.
She is a heavenly vision,
A dream most rare and tender,
Which, floating through earth's darkness,
Radiates celestial splendor.
Born in the public streets—
Oh, blind caprice of fate,
To trail through muddy streams
A flower so immaculate!

ESMERALDA (*fixing her eyes on* PHŒBUS *in the crowd*).
It is my Phœbus, I was sure,
Just as that night I found him;
Whether in satin or in steel,
How grace and strength surround him!
Phœbus—my head is all on fire,
All burns within me, joy and pain;
My soul's consumed for lack of tears,
Just as earth yearns for rain.

FLEUR-DE-LYS.
How fair she is—yes, I was sure!
Jealous, indeed, I ought to be;
But yet to match that loveliness
How great must be my jealousy!
Alas! perhaps we both, foredoomed
To waste 'neath sorrow's harsh caress,
Full soon shall die—she in her flower,
I in my loneliness!

MADAME ALOISE.
> A radiant creature, truly,
> But, faith, 'tis a disgrace
> That such a wretched gypsy
> Should have so sweet a face.
> Alas! the curious laws of fate
> 'Tis not for mortal mind to know:
> The serpent hides his treacherous head
> Beneath the fairest flowers that grow.

ALL (*together*).
> She has the calmness, the delight
> Of radiant skies on a warm night.

MADAME ALOISE (*to* Esmeralda).
> Come, child! My beauty, come—
> Come and dance us some new dance!

[ESMERALDA *prepares to dance, and draws from her bosom the scarf which* PHŒBUS *gave her.*]

FLEUR DE-LYS.
> My scarf! Phœbus, you have deceived me!
> My rival! Here she is!

[FLEUR-DE-LYS *snatches the scarf from* ESMERALDA, *and falls in a swoon. All the people rush angrily toward the gypsy, who flies for protection to* PHŒBUS.]

ALL.
> Is it true that Phœbus loves her?
> Infamous creature, go—depart!
> To brave us thus in our own home,
> You must have an audacious heart.
> Oh! height of insolence! Retire!
> Go back into the public street!

The common tradesmen, they can praise
The jumping of your low-born feet.
Away with her, away at once!
Out at the door! 'Tis a disgrace
For this degraded girl to lift
Her eyes to such a lofty place.

ESMERALDA.
Oh, defend me! Help! Defend me,
Save me, Phœbus, I implore thee;
For the poor forsaken gypsy,
Stands defenseless now before thee!

PHŒBUS.
I love her, and I love but her.
Yes! her defender I will be.
I'll fight for her, and my strong arm
Will bear my heart out valiantly.
If some one must be her protector,
I am the one—and doubt me not,
Her wrongs are mine, and who insults her
Must answer for it on the spot.

ALL.
What! She is what he loves! Indeed!
Away from here, away from here!
A gypsy he prefers to us;
With loving words he calms her fear.
Hush! silence! Both of you be still!
No further words of insolence.
[*To* PHŒBUS.] From you, 'tis too much arrogance!
[*To* ESMERALDA.] From thee, too much impertinence!
[PHŒBUS *and his friends protect the gypsy, who is menaced by*

all the guests of MADAME DE GONDELAURIER. ESMERALDA staggers toward the door.

ACT III

SCENE.—*The front yard of a tavern. Tavern to the right; trees to the left. In the back a door, and a small low wall which closes in the yard. In the distance the roof of Notre Dame with its towers and its spire. A dark silhouette of old Paris outlines itself against the red sunset. The river Seine is at the base of the picture*

SCENE I

PHŒBUS, VISCOUNT DE GIF, M. DE MORLAIX, M. DE CHEVREUSE, *and many other friends of* PHŒBUS, *seated at tables, are drinking, and singing; afterward* DON CLAUDE FROLLO

CHORUS.
Be propitious and well-inclined,
Our Lady of Saint Lo,
To him who only water hates
Of all things here below!
PHŒBUS.
Give to the brave

In every place
A well-filled cellar,
A pretty face.
Happy fellow!
Help him hold
Dainty women,
Wine that's old.

If a beauty
Of cold mien
Be unwilling,
'Tis sometimes seen,
He jokes with her
With merry winks,
Then he sings,
Then he drinks!

The day goes by.
Or drunk or not,
He soon embraces
His Toinotte;
Then ferocious
He goes to bed
In a cannon's mouth,
And sleeps like lead!

And his soul,
Which often seems
To mix up women
With his dreams,

Is contented if the wind,
With its come and go,
Rocks the canvas of his tent
Gently to and fro!

CHORUS.
Be propitious and well inclined,
Our Lady of Saint Lo!
To him who only water hates
Of all things here below.

[*Enter* CLAUDE FROLLO, *who seats himself at a table at some distance from* PHŒBUS, *and appears at first to observe nothing that passes around him.*

VISCOUNT DE GIF (*to* Phœbus).
That pretty gypsy,
What are you doing with her?

[CLAUDE FROLLO *makes a movement of attention.*

PHŒBUS.
To-night, in an hour,
I have a meeting with her.

ALL.
Truly?

PHŒBUS.
Truly!

[*The agitation of* CLAUDE FROLLO *increases.*

VISCOUNT DE GIF.
In one hour?

PHŒBUS.
In one moment!
Oh, love! supremest rapture!
To feel one heart holds two!

To own the woman that one loves—
Be slave and conqueror too!
To have her soul; to have her charms,
Her song which fills with bliss;
To see her sweet eyes wet with tears,
To dry them with a kiss.
[*While he sings, the others drink and strike their glasses.*
CHORUS.
'Tis a rapture supreme,
Whatever one thinks,
To drink to one's love,
And to love what one drinks!
PHŒBUS.
Friends, the prettiest of all,
A grace divine,
Oh, wonder, ecstasy!
Friends, she is mine!
CLAUDE FROLLO (*aside*).
I bind myself to hell;
Misfortune on you dwell!
PHŒBUS.
Pleasure awaits us;
Exhaust without remorse
The better part of life,
Love's precious intercourse!
What matter if one dies,
When joy has passed away,
I'd give a century for an hour,
Eternity for a day.
[*The curfew rings; the friends of* PHŒBUS *arise from the table,*

replace their swords, their caps, their cloaks, and prepare to depart.

CHORUS.
   Phœbus, the hour is come;
   It is the curfew-bell:
   Hurry to your beloved;
   God's blessing on you dwell!
PHŒBUS.
   At last the hour is come;
   It is the curfew-bell.
   I go to my beloved;
   God's blessing on her dwell!
   [*The friends of* PHŒBUS *go out.*

SCENE II

CLAUDE FROLLO, PHŒBUS. CLAUDE FROLLO *stops* PHŒBUS *as he is about to go out*

CLAUDE FROLLO.
   Captain!
PHŒBUS.
   Who is this man?
CLAUDE FROLLO.
   Listen to me?
PHŒBUS.
   Make haste!

CLAUDE FROLLO.

　Do you know the name of the one Who awaits you at the meeting to-night?

PHŒBUS.

　By my life, it is my beauty!
　The one I love and who loves me.
　My song-bird, my dancing gypsy,
　My Esmeralda, it is she!

CLAUDE FROLLO.

　It is death!

PHŒBUS.

　Friend! First, you are an idiot;
　Second, go to the devil!

CLAUDE FROLLO.

　Listen!

PHŒBUS.

　What do I care?

CLAUDE FROLLO.

　Phœbus, if you cross the threshold of that door—

PHŒBUS.

　You are mad!

CLAUDE FROLLO.

　You are dead!
　Tremble! One of the gypsies she!
　No law protects those awful places.
　There love's a masquerade for hate,
　Death lies concealed in their embraces.

PHŒBUS (*laughing*).

　My dear sir, readjust your cape,
　Return unto your fools' retreat!

Strange they allow you to escape!
May Esculapius, Jupiter, the Devil,
Thither conduct your straying feet!

CLAUDE FROLLO.

Truly they are faithless women;
Believe that the report speaks true.
Darkness strange and deep surrounds them;
Phœbus! there death waits for you!

[CLAUDE FROLLO's *earnestness seems to trouble* PHŒBUS, *who looks at his interrogator with anxiety.*

PHŒBUS.

He astounds me!
Ah, he wounds me,
In spite of myself, with doubt!
This city great
Is full of hate,
And treachery is all about!

CLAUDE FROLLO.

I astound him,
And I wound him,
In spite of himself, with doubt.
The fool, he fears,
And sees and hears
Nothing but treachery about.
Believe me—my lord, avoid the siren
Who lures you to destruction.
More than one gypsy in her rage
Has stabbed a heart palpitating with love.

[PHŒBUS, *whom he tries to drag along, recovers himself and pushes him off.*

PHŒBUS.
> Have I become a fool?
> Gypsy, Jewess, or Moor,
> The love that questions what she be
> Is love most base and poor.
> The fateful hour is come,
> Unto my love I fly!
> If death be but as sweet as she,
> It will be fine to die!

CLAUDE FROLLO (*holding him*).
> Consider! A gypsy!
> Your folly is great.
> How dare you thus rashly
> Trifle with fate!
> Oh, dread the false creature
> Who waits in the gloom,
> And do not thus wildly
> Rush to your doom.

[PHŒBUS *exits quickly, in spite of* CLAUDE FROLLO. CLAUDE FROLLO *stands gloomy and undecided for a moment; then follows* PHŒBUS.

SCENE III

A chamber. In the background, a window which opens on the river. CLOPIN FROUILLEFOU *enters, bearing a torch. He is followed by several men, to whom he makes a preconcerted sign, and places them in a dark corner, in which they disappear;*

then he returns to the door and signals to some one to come up.
Don Claude *appears*

CLOPIN (*to* Claude).
   From here you can see the captain
   And the gypsy without being seen.
   [*He shows him an alcove behind some tapestry.*
CLAUDE FROLLO.
   The men are stationed and ready?
CLOPIN.
   They are ready.
CLAUDE FROLLO.
   The projector of this must never be known.
   Silence! take this purse.
   I will give you as much more afterward.
   [Claude Frollo *hides himself in the alcove.* Clopin *exits with caution.* Esmeralda *and* Phœbus *enter.*
CLAUDE FROLLO (*aside*).
   Oh, woman adored,
   Destiny's prey!
   She enters in beauty,
   In tears goes away.
ESMERALDA (*to* Phœbus).
   My lord the count,
   My feelings I try to hide.
   My heart is filled with shame,
   And filled also with pride.
PHŒBUS (*to* Esmeralda).
   My beauty, white and red,
   I beg you blush no more.

Love, entering love's domain,
Leaves fear outside the door.
[PHŒBUS *makes* ESMERALDA *sit down on the bench beside him.*

PHŒBUS.
Dost thou love me?
ESMERALDA.
I love thee!
CLAUDE FROLLO (*aside*).
What torture!
PHŒBUS.
The adorable creature!
Upon my soul, you are divine!
ESMERALDA.
Your lips are flatterers;
You make me feel ashamed.
I beg of you, don't come so near.
CLAUDE FROLLO.
They love each other. How I envy them!
ESMERALDA.
My Phœbus! I owe my life to you.
PHŒBUS.
And I—I owe my happiness to you.
ESMERALDA.
Be good to me!
Oh, try to be
Gentle, I entreat,
To the young maid,
Who much afraid
Trembles at your feet!

PHŒBUS.

    Oh, my white queen,
    Goddess serene,
    Sovereign of beauty,
    Whose bright eyes shine
    With fires divine
    Of passion and of duty!

CLAUDE FROLLO.

    I wait for them;
    I hark to them.
    How tender she,
    How handsome he!
    How near their doom!
    Be joyous he,
    And happy she,
    While I prepare their tomb!

PHŒBUS.

    Nymph or woman,
    Saint or human,
    Be my wife to me!
    All day I yearn,
    All night I burn,
    Such is my love for thee!

ESMERALDA.

    I am woman,
    I am human,
    And my soul afire,
    Trembles ever,
    Longs forever,
    As throbs a lover's lyre!

CLAUDE FROLLO.
>   Woman, wait!
>   My flame as great,
>   My blade must have its turn.
>   Oh! I admire
>   These souls afire,
>   And these hearts which burn!

PHŒBUS.
>   Be always white and red, my love,
>   And smile at our bright lot;
>   Smile sweet at love, which we've awaked,
>   And chastity, which we've forgot.
>   Your mouth is heaven—my heaven, love—
>   My soul would cling in bliss
>   Upon it, love, and pray that life
>   Might end with one long kiss.

ESMERALDA.
>   Your voice delights my ear, love;
>   Your smile is sweet and free.
>   The laughing passion in your eyes
>   Benumbs and conquers me.
>   Your wishes are my law, love,
>   But I can't yield to this:
>   My virtue and my happiness
>   Might die in that long kiss!

CLAUDE FROLLO.
>   Don't let them hear your step, Death,
>   As near to them you creep!
>   My jealous hatred will keep watch
>   While their love falls asleep.

From out their arms so closely locked
You'll steal away their bliss!
Phœbus—your wish is granted,
You die for that long kiss!
[CLAUDE FROLLO *rushes upon* PHŒBUS *and stabs him; then he opens the window in the back, through which he escapes. With a great cry,* ESMERALDA *falls upon the body of* PHŒBUS. *The men stationed at the corner rush forward, seize her, and seem to accuse her.*

ACT IV

SCENE.—*A prison. Door in the center*

SCENE I

ESMERALDA (*alone, chained, lying upon a bed of straw*).
What! He in the tomb and I in this cell—
He a victim and I a prisoner!
I saw him fall! In truth, he's dead!
And this crime, this awful crime—
They say it is my work!
The stem of our life, while yet green, is broken.
Phœbus has gone, and he shows me the way.
Yesterday they made his grave,
To-morrow they'll make mine!

ROMANCE
>   Phœbus, is there nothing left,
>   No help given, to those bereft
>   In this cruel wise—
>   Neither filters, love, nor charms,
>   To assuage the soul's alarms,
>   Or reopen closèd eyes?
>
>   God in heaven, I adore thee!
>   Every hour I implore thee!
>   Deign to end my life to-day
>   Or to take my love away!
>
>   Phœbus, let us turn our wings
>   Toward the lights supernal,
>   Where all things must go at last,
>   Where love bides and is eternal.
>   On earth our bodies sleep together,
>   In heaven our souls will live forever!
>
>   God in heaven, I adore thee!
>   Every hour I implore thee!
>   Deign to end my life to-day
>   Or to take my love away!
>   [*The door opens.* CLAUDE FROLLO *enters, a lamp in his hand, his hood pulled over his face: he comes and stands, motionless, in front of* ESMERALDA.

ESMERALDA (*jumping up with terror*).
>   Who is this man?

CLAUDE FROLLO (*covered by his hood*).

   A priest!

ESMERALDA.

   A priest! How mysterious!

CLAUDE FROLLO.

   Are you ready?

ESMERALDA.

   Ready for what?

CLAUDE FROLLO.

   Ready to die.

ESMERALDA.

   Yes.

CLAUDE FROLLO.

   It is well.

ESMERALDA.

   Will it be soon? Answer me, father!

CLAUDE FROLLO.

   Do you suffer so much?

ESMERALDA.

   Yes, I suffer.

CLAUDE FROLLO.

   Perhaps I, who shall live to-morrow,
   Suffer more than you.

ESMERALDA.

   You? Who, then, are you?

CLAUDE FROLLO.

   The tomb lies between us!

ESMERALDA.

   Your name?

CLAUDE FROLLO.

You wish to know it?

ESMERALDA.

Yes. [*He lifts his hood.*

The priest!

It is the priest! O God! my feeble strength inspire!

It is indeed his brow of ice, it is his glance of fire!

'Tis he who has pursued me, remorseless, day and night;

'Twas he who killed my Phœbus, and slew my heart's delight.

Monster, from my prison, with death's cold hand on me,

I'll curse thee, till within the grave my lips shall silent be!

What have I done to thee? What is thine awful plan?

What dost thou want with me, relentless, impious man?

You hate me!

CLAUDE FROLLO.

I love you!

I love you—it is infamous!

Oh, shame to my priesthood!

This love, it is my soul;

This love, it is my blood!

At your feet I fall;

Hear my heart, which cries,

I prefer your tomb

Unto Paradise.

Pity me. I love you! Your pity I implore!

For you I've sinned. Have mercy, do not curse me more!

ESMERALDA.

He loves me! Oh, crown of horrors!

He holds me—this horrible sorcerer!

CLAUDE FROLLO.
　　The only living thing in me
　　Is my love and my anguish!
　　Hopeless anguish,
　　Wretched plight!
　　Alas! I love her,
　　Painful night!
ESMERALDA.
　　Awful moment,
　　Cruel fright!
　　Heaven! He loves me,
　　Fearful night.
CLAUDE FROLLO (*aside*).
　　She shudders, quivers in my arms;
　　The priest has won his chance at last!
　　By night I bore her, once, away;
　　Now, in the day, I'll hold her fast!
　　Death, which follows in my train,
　　Will give her back to love again!
ESMERALDA.
　　Pity—pity, let me go!
　　Phœbus is dead; he waits above.
　　Alas! I tremble, I'm afraid,
　　I shiver at your frightful love,
　　E'en as the bird which, tortured, dies
　　Beneath the vulture's cruel eyes!
CLAUDE FROLLO.
　　Accept me, I love you! Refuse me no more!
　　Have pity for me, for yourself, I implore!

ESMERALDA.
  Your prayer is an insult.
CLAUDE FROLLO.
  Would you rather die?
ESMERALDA.
  The body dies—the soul lives!
CLAUDE FROLLO.
  To die is terrible!
ESMERALDA.
  Hush! your impious words!
  Your love makes death beautiful!
CLAUDE FROLLO.
  Choose! choose! Or Claude or death!
  [Claude *falls at* ESMERALDA'S *feet in supplication. She repels him.*
ESMERALDA.
  No, murderer, I will not! Hush!
  A crime is this foul love you've nursed.
  Better the tomb to which I fly—
  Be cursed amid the most accursed!
CLAUDE FROLLO.
  Tremble, for the scaffold claims you!
  You know not what awful schemes
  This breast of fury has engendered;
  And hell abets me in my dreams.
  How I love thee!
  Thy hand give,
  And to-morrow
  Thou shalt live!
  Night benumbed

With terror's breath!
Tears for me,
For thee death!
Say, "I love thee!"
Cease thy scorning;
Thy last day
Is dawning!
Ah! since in vain I supplicate,
In vain thy hate I fight,
Farewell forever! One day more,
Then comes eternal night.

ESMERALDA.
Inhuman priest.
Go! I abhor thee!
His dear blood yet
Seems dripping o'er thee,
Oh, night of horror,
Night of shame!
Enough of tears;
Death I claim!
In prison I brave thee,
In chains defy!
Be thou accursed
Eternally!
Thy passion be thy punishment!
To God my love leads me:
The gates of heaven he'll open,
But hell shall close o'er thee!

[*A jailer appears.* CLAUDE FROLLO *signs to him to lead out* Esmeralda. *He exits while they drag forth the gypsy.*

SCENE II

The area before Notre Dame; the front of the church. The sound of bells is heard

QUASIMODO.
  My God! I love,
  Except myself,
  All that's here—
  The air which passes,
  And which chases
  Away care;
  And the swallow
  Who is faithful
  To the old roof;
  The chapels high
  O'ershadowed by
  The Holy Cross;
  Every rose
  That grows;
  Every sight
  Of delight!

  Sad creature, I—
  Uncouth, ill-made!
  None envies me!
  This is life
  As it is!
  Darkest night,

Bluest sky,
What matters it?
Every door
Leads to God.
Ignoble scabbard,
Noble blade;
Fair my soul
God has made.

Ring, bells small and great—
Ring on, ring on!
Mix well your voices,
Gruff and sweet!
In the turrets,
In the tower,
Sing your song!

How they ring!
With all their might,
Let them hum
Day and night!
Our festival shall be
Magnificent, I swear!
Assail it fiercer yet,
The palpitating air!
The stupid peasants run,
And o'er the bridges tear!

Let them ring,
Let them hum,

Day and night!
Every feast
Is increased
By their might!

[*He turns toward the front of the church.*
I saw black hangings in the chapel.
Are they dragging some misery here?
God! a presentiment! I'll not believe it!
[*Enter* CLAUDE FROLLO *and* CLOPIN *without perceiving*
QUASIMODO.
It is my master! I'll observe him. He is gloomy too!
[*He hides himself in an obscure angle of the porch.*
Oh, my mistress! Oh, Notre Dame!
Take my life! save my soul!

SCENE III

QUASIMODO *hidden,* CLAUDE FROLLO, CLOPIN

CLAUDE FROLLO.
  So Phœbus is at Montfort?
CLOPIN.
  My lord, he is not dead!
CLAUDE FROLLO.
  Provided nothing brings him here!
CLOPIN.
  Do not fear it;

He is too feeble yet for such a journey.
If he came, 'twould be his death.
My lord, you can feel sure
That every step would reopen his wound;
Do not fear anything this morning.

CLAUDE FROLLO.
Oh! let me hold her just to-day
For life or death within my power!
Hell! I'll give you all the rest,
If you grant me this one hour!
[*To* CLOPIN.] They will soon bring the gypsy here!
You remember everything!
In the square—with your men—

CLOPIN.
Yes.

CLAUDE FROLLO.
Keep in the shadow;
If I cry, "To me!" you come.

CLOPIN.
Yes!

CLAUDE FROLLO.
Have plenty with you!

CLOPIN.
If you cry, "To me!"

CLAUDE FROLLO.
Yes.

CLOPIN.
I rush to her,
I tear her from the King's men—

CLAUDE FROLLO.
   Yes.
CLOPIN.
   And give her to you.
CLAUDE FROLLO.
   Go, mix among the crowd,
   And perhaps she
   Will look upon the priest
   More tenderly;
   Then rush—rush all of you—
CLOPIN.
   Yes, my master!
CLAUDE FROLLO.
   Hold yourselves close!
CLOPIN.
   Yes.
CLAUDE FROLLO.
   Hide your arms,
   Not to excite suspicion!
CLOPIN.
   Master, you shall see!
CLAUDE FROLLO.
   But hell may take her quick,
   With my good-will,
   If now this insane creature
   Refuses still!

   Destiny! Oh, fatal stroke!
   Friend, I count on thee!
   On this my only chance I wait

With fierce anxiety.
CLOPIN.
Fear nothing terrible, my lord,
Count faithfully on me,
And on this last and only chance
Rely courageously!
[*They go out hurriedly. The populace begin to enter the square.*

SCENE IV

The populace; QUASIMODO; *afterward* ESMERALDA, *and her escort; then* CLAUDE FROLLO, PHŒBUS, CLOPIN FROUILLEFOU, *priests, archers, officers of the law*

CHORUS.
To Notre Dame
Come, get a sight
Of the young woman
Who dies to-night!

This gypsy woman
Who stabbed, they say,
The handsomest officer
In the King's pay.

In vain did Heaven
Beauty lend her!
Is it possible—

God defend her!—
A soul so black,
An eye so tender!

A frightful thing,
Human nature is so!
The poor unfortunate!
Come, let us go
To Notre Dame
To get a sight
Of the young woman
Who dies to-night!

[*The crowd increases; noise; a gloomy procession begins to appear on the Place du Parvis. Rows of black penitents. Banners of La Miséricorde. Torches, archers, officers of the law and the watch. The soldiers disperse the crowd.* ESMERALDA *appears. She wears a chemise; a rope is around her neck; her feet are bare, and she is covered with a long black veil of crape. Following her, come the executioners and the King's officers. As the prisoner reaches the front of the church, a somber chant is heard in the distance, coming from the interior of the church, whose doors are closed.*

CHORUS (*in the church*).
Omnes fluctus fluminis
Transierunt super me
In imo voraginis
Ubi plorant animæ.

[*The chant draws nearer. It bursts forth, at length, when near the doors, which open suddenly and discover the interior of the church. It is filled with a long procession of priests in their robes of ceremony; banners are borne before them.* CLAUDE FROLLO, *in sacerdotal costume, leads the procession. He goes toward the criminal.*

THE PEOPLE.
    Alive to-day, to-morrow dead!
    Heaven! thy wings around her spread!

ESMERALDA.
    It is Phœbus who calls me
    Unto our home eternal,
    Where God will hold us in His arms,
    Safe from misfortunes cruel.
    Though plunged in the abyss of woe,
    A joyful hope is given:
    I am to die upon the earth
    To be re-born in heaven!

CLAUDE FROLLO.
    To die so young, so beautiful!
    Alas! the guilty priest
    Must suffer greater woe than she;
    He ne'er will be released.
    Oh, hapless child of sorrow,
    Lost through my infamy,
    You only die from off this earth,
    While heaven is lost to me!

THE PEOPLE.
    Alas! she is an infidel.
    God's words, unto us spoken,
    Say that in heaven for such as she
    No blessed gate shall open.

Death holds her fast, what misery!
She can escape it, never!
She dies unto the world this day,
And unto heaven forever!
[*The procession approaches.* CLAUDE *accosts* ESMERALDA.

ESMERALDA (*frozen with terror*).

It is the priest!

CLAUDE FROLLO (*low*).

Yes, it is I! I love you, I entreat you!
Say but one word! 'Tis not too late;
I can yet save you!
Say, I love you!

ESMERALDA.

I abhor you! Go!

CLAUDE FROLLO.

Then die! I'll go where I can find you!
[Claude *turns to the crowd.*
We deliver this woman to the secular arm;
At this solemn moment may the breath of the Lord
Pass over her soul!
[*As the officers of the law are about to seize* ESMERALDA, QUASIMODO *jumps into the square, thrusts back the archers, takes* ESMERALDA *in his arms, and throws himself with her into the church.*

QUASIMODO.

Sanctuary! sanctuary! sanctuary!

THE PEOPLE.

Sanctuary! sanctuary! sanctuary!
Rejoice, O people!
Hail to the good bell-ringer!

Oh, destiny!
The criminal
Belongs to heaven!
The scaffold falls!
The eternal God
Instead of a tomb
Discloses the altar!
Executioners, back!
King's officers, back!
This barrier
Limits your power.
Thou hast changed
Everything here.
The angels claim her;
She belongs to God!

CLAUDE FROLLO (*commanding silence by a gesture*).
She is not saved! She is a gypsy!
Notre Dame can save none but Christians!
Pagans are proscribed even when clasping the altar!
[*To the King's men.*] In the name of my lord the Archbishop of Paris,
I give you back this sinful woman!

QUASIMODO (*to the archers*).
I will defend her! I swear it.
Approach us not!

CLAUDE FROLLO (*to the archers*).
Do you hesitate?
Obey me, on the instant!
Tear the gypsy from this holy place.

[*The archers advance.* QUASIMODO *places himself between them and* ESMERALDA.

QUASIMODO.
  Never!
[*A horseman is heard approaching. He calls out*:
  Wait! [*The crowd disperses.*
PHŒBUS (*appearing on horseback. He is pale, breathless, exhausted as is a man who has made a long journey*).
  Wait!
ESMERALDA.
  Phœbus!
CLAUDE FROLLO (*aside, terrified*).
  My plot has failed.
PHŒBUS (*leaping from his horse*).
  God be praised! I breathe
  And I arrive in time!
  This girl is innocent.
  Behold my assassin!
  [*Points to* CLAUDE FROLLO.
ALL.
  Heavens! the priest!
PHŒBUS.
  The priest alone is guilty, and I will prove it!
  Arrest him!
THE PEOPLE.
  Oh, wonder!
  [*The archers surround* CLAUDE FROLLO.
CLAUDE FROLLO.
  God alone is Master!

ESMERALDA.

Phœbus!

PHŒBUS.

Esmeralda!

[*They fall into each other's arms.*

ESMERALDA.

My adored Phœbus, we shall live!

PHŒBUS.

Thou shalt live!

ESMERALDA.

For us shines happiness!

THE PEOPLE.

Live, both of you!

ESMERALDA.

Hear these joyous shouts!

At thy feet receive me, humble girl!

Heavens! thou art pale! What is the matter?

PHŒBUS (*staggering*).

I die!

[*She catches him in her arms. Expectation and anxiety among the crowd.*

Each step I took toward you, my beloved,

Reopened my wound, that was hardly healed.

I have taken your grave and given you life.

I die! Destiny has avenged thee.

My angel, I go to see

If heaven is worth thy love!

Farewell! [*He dies.*

ESMERALDA.

Phœbus! He dies! In an instant everything is changed!

[*She falls upon his body.*
I follow you into eternity.
CLAUDE FROLLO.
Fatality!
THE PEOPLE.
Fatality!

www.ingramcontent.com/pod-product-compliance
Lightning Source LLC
Chambersburg PA
CBHW031325230426
43670CB00006B/242